LOVING
THE
UNLOVABLE

Transforming Difficult Relationships with God's Truth

KIRSTEN STRAWN

The Faith Coach
San Diego, California

LOVING THE UNLOVABLE
Published by The Faith Coach
San Diego, CA U.S.A.

Kirsten would love to hear from you. Please contact her through her website at
www.thefaithcoach.com. May the God of comfort and compassion bless you with His
peace, presence, and divine revelation as you read this book.

© 2013 Kirsten Strawn
www.thefaithcoach.com

Cover Photo by Nito
Author Photo by Ashley McGrew
Cover Design by Suzanne West

ISBN-10: 0988847000
ISBN-13: 978-0-9888470-0-2

Library of Congress Control Number: 2013930680
1.Religion 2.Christian Living 3.Relationships

The Faith Coach
Printed in the United States of America
First Edition 2013

Dedicated to my heavenly Father,

Thank you for loving me,
even when I'm unlovable.

What people are saying about *Loving The Unlovable*:

This is a great book to read now, and then refer back to again and again, as a valuable life-tool and reference guide. Wendy W.

If you're looking for answers, if you've had great pain and you struggle, or if you just want to improve the quality of your life, I highly recommend reading this book. Laura N.

Part of what sets Kirsten's writing apart is her gift for combining her own personal experiences, the testimony of people she's met along her life's journey and practical steps to help you transform your thinking in order to allow God to move in your relationships. Tami M.

This is such a powerful book on how to love like Jesus loved. This book is one that I would recommend to everyone. The scripture references are so powerful and the challenges at the end of each chapter help you to go deeper. Teresa H.

This book has transformed my relationships. I was able to change my heart and begin to love that difficult person in my life. The steps were helpful in changing my actions and seeing others perspective. Christine S.

This book provided me with a positive outlook that has changed my life in many ways. Jennifer C.

My faith has been lifted to a new level and I'm in expectation for God's complete redemptive power in my life as well. Beverly B.

This book transformed my life. It made me look at myself in a better light and look at people without judging them. Rosy

With personal accounts of herself, family, and friends' stories, Kirsten takes us on a journey of enlightenment to forgiveness, to living free in Christ. Laura W.

Awesome book and a great read. Chapter after chapter I'm learning more and more…about me and what areas of life I need to work on. E. L. Viana

Thank you Kirsten for taking the time, the energy, the prayer and for persevering in writing this book! It is a blessing! Karen S.

This book is amazing! It is filled with transforming Truth and revelation. I have learned so much about myself, my husband and the people in my life. I am empowered with tools for divine relationships. Doris D.

This is a wonderful book for anyone who is feeling hurt or overwhelmed by past pain and find that they are unable to find a way to let go. M. Grady

I'm in awe at how God is using these truths shared by Kirsten to transform my thinking. In fact, I gained insight on how to speak truth in love to my mother and put up some healthy boundaries in that relationship. Michele M.

Throughout the book, you feel every experience, as if you are standing beside the author, watching each scene unfold. The encouragement and revelations throughout this book are life changing. S. Hover

Acknowledgments

My sincere appreciation goes to my committed husband, Mark, who persevered so we could see God's plan through the pain. My complete opposite, Mark has inspired and supported my 16-year journey to bring this book to completion. Although frustrated at times with the lengthy process, he continued to encourage me to stay dedicated to accomplish my goal to help others learn what took us years to attain. Grateful to my precious children: Kayla, Kylie, Connor, and Cameron who are a gift from God. They have shown me grace as I have struggled to balance motherhood as a writer, Evangelist, and Faith Coach. Thankfully my family has allowed me to be transparent to testify to God's power at work in our lives.

With a grateful heart, I thank my mom and dad who brought me into this world to begin my journey to discover love. Thanks for allowing me to share our struggles for the purpose to bring hope and healing to others. A special thanks to my mom and my stepdad, Bill, who are two of my biggest advocates. They provided the finances to publish this book as well as make me feel loved and adored every day.

Eternally grateful for my bold and courageous sister, Karen, who had the guts to tell me she saw through my pretenses and that I needed God. Because of her, many lives have been saved. Thanks to my twin brother, Craig, and his wife, Wendy. They kept me light-hearted with their great sense of humor and encouragement during our coffee-time.

Thanks to my sisters and brothers in Christ who testify to the power of God through this book. Pamela who was the first to show me what it meant to walk with Jesus and love like Him. Mel and Latisha, Stacy, Gail, Janine, Dottie, Patty, Kenji and Charlene, Jamie, Steve, and Kent thank you for sharing your testimony to demonstrate the power of God. To protect families, some of these names have been changed. Ever so grateful to my spiritual family who has encouraged me along my journey, prayed for me, held me accountable, and reminded me that they needed this book. Thanks to my friends Anita Palmer, Michele Richardson, Mishe Harvey, Missee Allen, Stephanie Hover, Michele McCormack, John Darrow, Greg Lloyd, and the others who contributed feedback during the editing process. Thanks to my friend Kathie who gave me the title for this book as she shared her insight on her journey to love the unlovable.

Appreciative to the many pastors and authors who preached God's Word and wrote books that inspired my love for Jesus, His Word, and His people. I'm grateful to pastor Mickey Stonier who ministers compassion to hurting people and equips others to do the same. Thankful that he created the acrostic, STOP, and encouraged me to share it with you. And a special thanks to my pastor, Miles McPherson, who boldly proclaims God's transforming truth every week and empowers his congregation to "Do Something" to change our world and demonstrate the love of Jesus.

Thanks to you, my friend, for allowing me to come into your life through the reading of this book. My heart longs for you to have peace and joy in your relationships. I have prayed for you, and will continue to pray, that through the following pages you will have a spirit of revelation to the transforming truth that will set you free to experience true love.

Contents

Introduction

Perhaps you opened this book because you're fed-up and ready to give up on a difficult relationship. Maybe you struggle with a critical parent that won't accept you for who you are. Or perhaps you're dealing with a troubled teen, a stubborn spouse, or worse yet, an enraged ex. Regardless of the source of your pain, I'm here to bring you hope.

You see, I understand it's easy to let your frustration turn to hatred, hopelessness, and despair. I did. Those thoughts and feelings are common. We all struggle with fear and anger and *what ifs*, thinking life would be better if that unlovable person was out of our life. But consider this, *what if* that person is in your life for a purpose? *What if* God wants to use this challenging person to give you an abundant life? Is it possible? I never thought so, until recently.

In the process of writing this book I was on the brink of divorce. I felt like a hypocrite. Miserable in my marriage I saw an attorney, paid the retainer fee, and was ready to file the papers for separation. Both my husband and I had had enough. I was in pain and I didn't know what else to do. Although I was teaching the principles you'll learn in this book, I was not fully living by them. I thought the only way to make my husband change was to make him pay, but God had something else in mind. When I applied biblical truths, God took my relationship from misery to immeasurably more than I could ask or imagine. And the same can be true for you.

If you're shouting, "No more pain!" then it's time to stop doing what you've been doing and try something new. Even if you're unsure whether working on the relationship will help, you may be willing to keep an open heart to God's Word and His encouragement. God may be gently nudging you to consider a different perspective. If you're ready for God to rock your foundation and have Him swing open the prison doors and take off the shackles like He did for Paul and Silas, then this book is for you.

Loving the Unlovable will give you truth to transform your relationship with God and with the people placed right before you in your home, workplace, church, and community. Let's face the fact that loving those people you can barely tolerate isn't easy. However, I guarantee the transforming truths outlined in the following chapters will challenge you to invite God into the depths of who you are, so that you can have a deeper capacity to be filled with God's love for you, which is what gets shared with others. Applying God's truth will set you free to love even the most difficult person.

Does this mean you become a doormat? Absolutely not! A life of loving God and others requires that you respect yourself as well. God wants you to be all that He has created you to be: confident, joyful, and peaceful, which makes love possible in the midst of the struggle. Oh yes, you'll still have struggles with unlovable people, but you'll handle them differently because you'll be empowered by God.

Chapter Structure:

The structure of this book includes twelve chapters that contain a biblical truth illustrated with a true story from my life, the Bible, and/or the lives of others. Included at the end of each chapter is a heartfelt prayer for you to pray, a truth highlighted along with a question to ponder in your heart, and an action step to take toward improving your difficult relationship.

Keep a Journal:

Read each chapter slowly with an open mind asking God to speak to you. Consider writing your thoughts and insights down in a journal for later reflection. Write down scriptures to meditate upon and receive the blessings that God promises when you do (Psalm 1:1-3). Also record your specific prayers to document the desires of your heart, so that you may later see God's faithfulness. Use your journal to truthfully answer the question that follows each chapter along with thoughts on how to accomplish the action step. Feel free to express yourself and don't worry about what you write. Your journal is a place to be honest and transparent. It's for your eyes only until you're ready to share.

Spiritual Family:

To become whole and healed, the person God desires you to be, I encourage forming a small group of two or more people through your church or community to work through these transforming truths. God created the church to do life together. Each individual contributes their gifts and talents to form a body that functions as a spiritual family. Gather together to work through the 12-week Bible study using the discussion questions at the end of the book. We learn from one another and are encouraged by the testimonies, godly wisdom, and prayers that we share. Community groups are not a gripe session, but a place to gain hope of true healing for your difficult relationship. Our lives are enriched through God's people who are the hands and feet of Jesus. Step out in faith to gather with others who are looking for tools to love challenging people. Together you will be encouraged and strengthened to love, even the most unlovable.

Loving the Unlovable

Chapter One

Come Out of Hiding

If we walk in the light, as He is in the light, we have
fellowship with one another, and the blood of
Jesus, His Son, purifies us from all sin.
1 John 1:7

Rejected people react in unlovable ways. Even the fear of rejection will lead people to be rude and aloof in an effort to protect their hearts from those who may reject them. The desire to be accepted compels many of us to compromise what's right to do whatever it takes to be loved.

Criticism, control, and complacency push spouses into divorce court or the arms of lovers. Conflict prompts between 1.6 and 2.8 million youth under the age of eighteen to leave home every year.[1] Unwed teens and young women who live in fear of rejection, confrontation, and the unknown run to abortion clinics. Hopeless, rejected people attempt to end their lives through drugs, alcohol, and suicide every day. Desperate to be accepted within the walls of our homes and communities we fight for love, runaway to find it, and sometimes give-up completely.

This is my story. Is it yours?

From the beginning of time the Bible has recorded stories of rejected people fighting or fleeing conflict from unlovable people. Consider Cain who felt rejected after he offered his leftover vegetables to God. Lashing out in bitterness and envy, Cain killed his brother Abel who was favored by God for his pure heart. Taking matters into his own hands, Jacob, ran from his angry older twin brother, Esau, after deceiving their father and stealing his brother's inheritance. Bitterness and fear kept them apart for nearly twenty years. Then there was Jonah, who due to his pride avoided preaching the saving grace of God to the wicked people of Nineveh. God grabbed hold of his heart in the belly of a fish to face his adversary and bring a city to God. And then Moses, a Hebrew baby rescued from death and adopted into the royal family of Egypt, as a young man murdered an Egyptian slave-master to protect his own. He fled with fear until the day God equipped him with courage to speak truth to the powerful Pharaoh that rescued his people out of slavery.

At some point in our lives, each of us has been rejected, neglected, abandoned, used, or abused. It's sad but true. Our parent's choices and the choices of others have impacted us. Choices we have made impacted our own lives and those in our sphere of influence. We camouflage our pain through power and pride. Proper behavior, appearance, education, economic status, or position influence the way in which we act toward others. Our comparisons lead us to believe we're better. We justify our sin of pride believing we're not as bad as *them*. Yet our common denominator when you strip away the make-up, the tight abs or extra weight, the money and power is that we all hurt. Our pain runs deep beneath our pretenses.

Walls of self-preservation can keep us distant and detached from experiencing true intimacy in our relationships. By coming out of the darkness of our painful past and present circumstances we become real. Similar to the darkness of a room exposed to the light, the darkness vanishes and we can finally see everything in that room clearly. In the same way, the light of truth can shine on the shame that keeps you hidden in the crevices of your insecurities. You no longer have to be afraid to be known. You can finally be authentic and experience true love. Without shame, you can become the person God created you to be. The Bible says,

If we walk in the light, as He is in the light, we have fellowship with one another, and the blood of Jesus, His Son, purifies us from all sin (1John 1:7).

When we are guarded and hiding in sin or the embarrassment of our past, we cannot truly walk in the light and love of Jesus. We miss out on genuine relationships when we live with secrets. Exposing our pain allows us to have true communion with one another, even with the most difficult people in our lives.

My wounds kept me hidden in the depths of my disgrace afraid to give my heart away, not willing to completely trust anyone, not even my husband. What about you? Are you avoiding conversations that are uncomfortable in fear of being judged or shot down? Do you long for acceptance but insecurities from past rejection keep you guarded and distant, paralyzed and unable to completely be free to love and be loved?

The inability to communicate our pain effectively causes the destruction of lives to continue. Until one day, we make the choice to acknowledge the place long ago that cries out to be heard. By acknowledging our place of rejection and betrayal we allow God to mend our brokenness through His people. He grows in us the ability to create real and authentic relationships that empower us to love difficult people from a new perspective, from the heart of God. With transparency, I share my story so you might remember your place of pain that keeps you hiding from the love that God has for you.

Hiding from Rejection

Growing up as a little girl, my father's addictions took my family down a road of destruction. Unfaithful to my mother, we paid the price of my father's infidelity. Quietly, I felt rejected when my father remained riveted on other women. There was no concealing his lust for the flesh with his comments about big breasts. When I started developing I felt flawed, inadequate, and insignificant. I wanted implants as soon as I could have them. I longed to be loved by my father, to be beautiful, and to be accepted by men.

By seventh grade I began experimenting with drugs and alcohol to bury the pain of rejection from parents who focused on their careers and other people instead of me. I longed to be seen and to be known. I concealed my pain behind well-applied make-up to make my nose straighter, my lashes longer, and I enhanced my cleavage with a well-padded bra to be accepted.

After my mother discovered my father's infidelity for the second time, my mother turned to a marriage and family workshop for help. Instead of finding refuge she found a counselor, Tom, who saw her as an easy target for his own selfish desires. My mother was a dynamic and beautiful professional woman, but vulnerable and desperate for love and acceptance. Tom captured her heart with his British charm and the attention she desperately longed for that ultimately won her over. She became putty in his hands.

This time her heart hardened toward my father whose betrayal crushed any trust that had been previously restored during a separation five years earlier. The possibility of saving her marriage ended with the strength of another man who wooed her off her feet. It didn't take much. My father had let his career, women, and alcohol consume him for most of his twenty years of marriage.

Tom stood beside my mother encouraging the divorce. His constant need for her time felt like love to her. He slithered his way into our lives, only to wreak havoc through his manipulation and control. Jealous for my mother's attention, he detested me. I saw it in his eyes and the way he caused trouble. To him, I was a distraction and an annoyance; I was a teenage girl interfering with *his* life with *my* mom.

At sixteen I sat alone the night my virginity was stolen by my girlfriend's older brother. Earlier that night, I had called my friend to cry on her shoulder about the break-up with my boyfriend, Eddie, when she wasn't there. Unexpectedly, her brother Josh answered the phone and invited me over. Flattered and anxious, my heart palpated when Josh greeted me at his front door like a gentleman. His dark wavy hair had grown out from the military crew cut he had when I last saw him. I relaxed when he offered me a glass of wine. He listened to my tale, told me what I needed to hear, but never listened to my no.

After Josh pushed his way into me, he prepared to go out for the evening with his adult friends. During the car ride home, he explained that I was too young to go to the club, but still I hoped for a kiss. Instead he simply said, "See ya," and that's when I knew he didn't love me. Confused by Josh's rejection and cool disdain for me, I subconsciously vowed that I would never be dumped at my doorstep again. I would be good enough that men would want me.

My parent's divorce was not a custody battle but a war on who got what possessions. I thought *does anybody want me?* Rejected by my dad and my mother, by Josh who stole my innocence and by Eddie who left me for his ex-girlfriend, until he wanted me back and I returned to him, I needed *someone* to love me. Life became difficult with Tom around. When I asked my father, he rejected my idea to live with him giving the excuse that he couldn't raise a daughter when he traveled for business. It made sense to me, but it still hurt.

I chose to move out of the house at sixteen to live with a friend named Lisa and her mother. My mother let me go. Within months, Tom pushed my fourteen-year-old sister out of the house to live with my dad. My father had no choice but to allow her to live with him. My twin brother, Craig, remained at home but spent most of his time away from the demands of my mother and her controlling boyfriend. At the same time, I had no rules or supervision at my friend's house. With my freedom I was failing most of my classes in tenth grade. I needed a fresh start. This time my dad agreed that I could come live with him and my sister. I left Lisa behind to move two hours south to a new city, with a new school, and a second chance to bring up my grades and make something of my life.

Soon after we moved in with my dad, his jealous girlfriend moved in and it became clear that she wanted us out. Through the walls of our rented house we could hear yelling, pushing, and broken glass that ricocheted off the wall to slit my father's throat. At the hospital the doctor said he was a lucky man. The shard of glass barely missed my father's artery, nevertheless we returned to the chaos. The girlfriend remained and every Friday night my boyfriend, Eddie, rescued me for the weekend. He became my savior.

After the school year ended, while my father and his girlfriend were away, Karen and I left the chaos to return to our hometown. I wasn't sure where I would live, but I knew there was no way I would go back to mother's house with her boyfriend still there. Karen wanted to live with my mom, but Tom refused. That weekend my mother put her on a bus to go back to my dad's.

She never arrived.

Hiding in Fear

That summer I stayed with a wonderful family as a nanny. Sitting on the floor in front of their TV, I saw my sister's face on the evening news as they reported her missing. Tears filled my eyes as I feared what might happen to her. I blamed my mom. Angry that she chose Tom over us, I wanted nothing to do with her.

Later I came to understand that my mother, not in her right mind, was a victim of isolation and intimidation. She knew that the choices she had made were contrary to her Christian teaching, however she didn't know what to do. Feeling ashamed of her behavior she chose not to seek help from our church in fear of judgment and condemnation.

Like a hostage in her own home, my mother was afraid for her life, and for what Tom might do to destroy the property or force her last child out of the house. It all came to a head when my twin brother, Craig, stepped in to defend our mother. With a baseball bat held high, he shouted at Tom, "Get out of our house!"

Seeing the rage in Craig's face, my mother's boyfriend left. My mother, weary from the battle with this selfish man, found the courage and confidence to end that abusive relationship. Shortly afterwards, before my junior year of high school, I left the nanny position to return home to live with my mother.

Meanwhile, Karen was still missing.

Four months went by without hearing from Karen. My mother hired a detective but we had no leads to go on. Each day that passed our hope diminished. We never talked about my sister thinking it would make it easier. I stayed busy with school and seeking the love and attention of my boyfriend.

One day I answered the phone to hear a familiar voice.

"Kirsten, it's me."

All my pent-up fears flowed down my cheeks, I sobbed, "Karen, you're alive! Are you alright?"

"I'm fine. I need to ask you a question."

I tried to pull myself together taking a deep breath, "What?" Standing at the kitchen window I stared at the bamboo hedges surrounding our well-manicured property that had failed to protect us from the outside world. The pretense of our perfect family had crumbled.

"Kirsten, do you think Mom will let me come home if I'm pregnant?"

Without hesitation I answered, "Yes. Of course! We want you home. Where are you?"

I promised to pick her up that night, getting directions before I hung up. When my mother and my boyfriend got off work, we drove eight hours, arriving at the small rundown motel around midnight. We pulled up to the room not knowing what to expect.

Karen answered the door with her suitcase in hand. Her blond listless hair fell around her dull blue eyes, framed by her high cheekbones. She looked like our mother. Three years younger than me, she was at least four inches taller and could pass for twenty-one.

We quickly put her luggage in the car, concerned that the father of her baby might show up at any moment to stop her from leaving.

He never came.

Relieved to have my sister safely with us, I probed for answers. She shut me down and told me to mind my own business. Karen stared out the dark window ignoring my mother's attempts to reconnect. We headed home in silence, my mother and Karen cramped in the back seat of the two-door Toyota, separated by a wall of resentment from the choices they had made.

We all had run away.

In the days that followed, family members strongly urged Karen to have an abortion to eliminate the problem, but she refused. Instead, Karen gave birth to an adorable baby boy who stole our hearts with his beautiful smile, dark sparkling eyes, and his loving spirit. The father of the baby was twenty years older than my sister. He had provided her shelter, but taken advantage of her. He stayed in Los Angeles with his girlfriend and the child they had together, showing little interest in the son he had with my sister. Believing she was in love, my sister was brokenhearted by his rejection. Wanting a father for her baby Karen eventually married an older man similar to my father's charming personality and with the same addictions. Comfortable felt normal. Years later their relationship crumbled with his drinking and infidelity.

Back when I was in high school, after my sister had her baby, I decided before my senior year to move in with my boyfriend Eddie, longing to create a home of my own. Even though he was unfaithful, smoked, drank, and had no ambition for his life, I clung to him. My mother had never stopped me from living with him, but after six months she finally had the courage to confront me. She told me I was a special young lady; she loved me and wanted the best for me. She insisted I move back home because I deserved better than Eddie. My mother's loving words changed the direction of my life. Finally, with great difficulty I ended that unhealthy relationship, but only because Eddie quickly replaced me with another girl.

After another year and a half with a man ten years older than me, who couldn't commit or say the words *I love you,* I met Mark. He was my math teacher in the community college I attended. When the summer class ended I asked him out thinking he would be fun to date. He made algebra tolerable for the first time with his enthusiasm and witty sense of humor. Within a few weeks of dating him I found myself at Planned Parenthood. The words, "You're pregnant," caught me off guard. I thought, *How could this happen? I've been on the pill for years.*

The nurse shook her head. "Obviously, you didn't plan for this pregnancy. And I'm sure you want to finish college and have a career," she said, looking at my paperwork, noting that I was twenty and not married. "Honey, you have your whole life ahead of you. It's just a fetus. You can take care of this problem by having an abortion."

When I told Mark the news, he was calm. He supported my right to choose, and warned me that I would be unable to accomplish my education and career goals if I had the baby. Remembering that my parents pushed for my sister to have an abortion, and unsure if I wanted to be with Mark, I decided to end the pregnancy. Soon afterwards I plunged into a deep depression that impacted my future decisions. Emotionally I detached, unable to connect with people in college. I felt alone and isolated, different from others.

It was about a year later that Mark, my no-nonsense, practical, and analytical boyfriend saw an opportunity to save money on his taxes and at the same time marry the girl of his dreams. He popped the most important question of my life, but I didn't understand the significance at the time. Still in a depression from the abortion, I felt obligated to marry Mark. He supported me. We had recently moved to San Diego and he offered everything I thought I needed: security, dependability, and constant attention.

For tax reasons, Mark wanted to elope before the end of the year but I was in love with the idea of a wedding, celebrated with family and friends. To have that wedding with delighted guests, we decided to keep our elopement a secret from everyone. I thought if we were secretly married, I could secretly divorce him if it didn't work out. I managed to get out of my depression by delving into my career.

A year and a half later we were married in front of family and friends under the pretense that it was our first wedding. Our marriage was based on secrets, the death of our first child, living with my instructor, elopement, and lies. I buried my feelings and kept peace every way I knew how.

Mark bragged that he had the perfect wife.

Hiding through Pride

The perfect wife worked endless hours to become successful and prove her self-worth. The classy clothes, make-up, power, and prestige of being a Nordstrom buyer became my identity. Flying to New York City every six weeks gave me purpose. Back to work after a six-week maternity leave, I left my first-born daughter Kayla at home with a nanny. Nineteen months later our second daughter Kylie was born.

Within four months I discovered that I was as good as my sinking sales figures. When my supervisor demoted me, my pride kept me from stepping down to a lower ranked position and I left the company. Later on, I realized that when I lost my job I lost my identity and the façade that I hid behind.

Within months of being at home with my children, I searched for a new identity outside of motherhood. Not understanding the important role that I had been entrusted with, I started a clothing business, and then a gift-basket business. Although I received validation from delighted customers, my time away from my husband and our four children caused conflict in my marriage. To create peace and uphold my agreement to stay home and raise our children, I ended my businesses and shifted my focus to decorating our new home. The phrase, *"shop 'til you drop,"* described me perfectly, yet I never dropped. At this point, I dragged my children around the stores on a treasure hunt, not realizing they were the treasure.

Once, my four-year-old daughter looked up at me with her big blue eyes and said, "Mommy, you love this house more than you love me." I couldn't understand why I was numb when I looked into the eyes of my precious children. I never slowed down to enjoy them. The house needed to be picture perfect, I needed to keep busy, and naturally I followed in my mother's footsteps until I found healing.

My sister came to visit me in San Diego from Northern California. For the first time she saw the chaos in my home with four children under the age of six and the problems in my marriage. One night as I struggled with my defiant six-year-old daughter, Karen said, "You don't have the perfect life and the perfect marriage like you portray. You've got major problems. Why don't you have a glass of wine to relax?"

I poured a glass of wine and mellowed, but it frightened me. I saw how drinking that one glass helped me to change my behavior toward Kayla, my strong-willed daughter. I knew that my father depended on alcohol to cope with his pain, and how it had reinforced his path of infidelity, divorce, and unmet dreams. I never wanted to rely on a substance like drugs or alcohol. But what else could help?

Karen also said, "You need God in your life." She insisted we attend church that weekend. After so many years of running from God, I finally found the Father's love I was searching for. There was a peace that I felt being back in church after eighteen years. I discovered that God welcomed me with open arms, that He still loved me, and He wanted a relationship with me.

Ironically, three weeks later I met my neighbor, Pamela. She was a wonderful Christian woman. An instant friendship grew as we began to walk five days a week. For the first time, I opened up and shared about my struggles and the pain of my past. She shared about forgiving her ex-husband who had committed adultery with her good friend that he later married. Astonished by the grace she extended to both of them and the love she poured out on me and my children, I was inspired to seek God in a deeper way.

Hiding through Pretense

I joined Pamela's Bible study where I met more amazing women who were transparent about their failures. Seeking to be better, they studied the Word of God, prayed together, and encouraged one another. For years I had put on pretenses that kept me distant from others. In the months that followed I exposed my sin to the light and experienced authentic relationships for the first time. I met Jesus at the well of my empty heart where I longed to be filled with His love.

God removed my mask.

To heal we must want to remove the mask. Many people, especially women, are guilty of pouring out all their past and present junk like emotional vomit with no intention of getting well or cleaning up the mess. We must be serious about not dwelling in the pain. Instead, we must confess our sins and the injustices committed against us so we can be forgiven, cleansed, and move past the ache in our hearts. Once healed, restored, and regenerated we become the beautiful creation God intended when He knit us together in the depths of our mother's womb.

God knows you intimately. He knows the number of hairs on your head (Matthew 10:30). He is aware of your pain. He wants to heal you and make you whole. The question is *do you want to heal?* To love the unlovable you must be healed from the times when you were unloved, rejected, and betrayed. To accept love from others you must allow God to enter in to love you and heal the depths of your soul. Healing can be a painful process, but it's worth the outcome for it is only when you experience the pain that you are set free to experience authentic love.

A Samaritan Woman's Testimony

Do you know the story of the woman at the well? Read her story in the fourth chapter of the Gospel of John. She was an outcast. Hiding from the townspeople, she went to the well to draw water in the heat of the day when no other women were around. She avoided the sneers and glares of those who judged her. Most everyone in her town knew she had been married five times and was now with a man who was not her husband.

We don't know her family history except that she was a Samaritan. Samaritans were a mixed race hated by the Jews. Nevertheless Jesus, a Jew and a Rabbi, stopped to talk to this woman. Bear in mind that it was not only unacceptable to talk to a Samaritan, but men and especially a teacher of the law like Jesus, were not allowed to speak to women in public. Jesus crossed all barriers to make a woman who lived in shame feel special. Jesus accepted her, not judging or condemning her, but extending His warm and gentle friendship. He knew everything about her, yet He still talked to her. He offered her living water to heal her pain and give her a life of freedom. A relationship with Him would quench the thirst of her soul. The woman was delivered from her shame. We know this to be true because after her encounter with Jesus she immediately ran to the townspeople she once had avoided to proclaim that she had met the Messiah. God used this restored woman to share her testimony to lead many in the town to Jesus.

Although never married five times, I related to the rejected woman. By the age of twenty, I had lived with three different men. I hid in shame. Back in high school, teachers and students gossiped that I lived with my boyfriend. I was the girl whose parents were divorced, whose fourteen-year-old sister had run away and who was now the mother of a baby boy. After I eloped, humbly I had to explain to the personnel manager at Nordstrom that I was secretly married to get the tax credit. To everyone else, I lived with my boyfriend. Shame consumed me and I felt judged.

My life changed when I stopped to talk to Jesus. He listened. He saw me. He knew my pain and everything about me. As I poured out my secrets into the light and love of Jesus, He healed me from the choices that were supposed to give me freedom. His compassion embraced me as He washed me with His Living Water. I no longer had to live in my past. No longer afraid of being judged, I was set free from my shame to share openly for the purpose to help others heal. God gave my life meaning as I began to take His Word seriously and walk with Him. Consider the following verses:

Let us throw off everything that hinders and the sin that so easily entangles, and let us run with perseverance the race marked out for us. Let us fix our eyes on Jesus, the author and perfecter of our faith, who for the joy set before Him endured the cross, scorning its shame, and sat down at the right hand of the throne of God (Hebrews 12:1-3).

The shame that entangles you is the shame that Jesus endured on the cross. He took it all. Every embarrassing, humiliating, and terrifying moment was His to tolerate. The rejection of your parents, friends, teachers, and those who used you for their own self-gratification rested upon His shoulders. He wore your robe of unrighteousness. Your selfishness, pride, bitterness, scared, and rebellious heart covered Him in blood. He knows your every flaw, insecurity, and painful moment. He saw every injustice committed against you as well as what you committed against others. His heart was broken as evil had its way with you through the precious gift of free choice. We turned our back on His love. We broke His heart and He still loves us. Jesus pursues us. Looking back, He put several Christians in my life as He patiently waited for me to accept His death on my behalf. What about you, has He been tugging on your heart? For you are the joy set before Jesus that empowered Him to go to the cross. If you don't know Him, Jesus wants to meet you right where you are. You don't need to be perfect, or know all the right answers, or even be sure of your faith. Simply stop to talk to Jesus to find His overwhelming love and acceptance. Let your wounds and scars be exposed to His light. Pray the following prayer with me:

Jesus, my Savior and Friend, I come out of hiding to meet you at the well of my soul. You know my pain, the burdens of my heart, the sins committed against me, and the sins I have committed. Let me throw off the sin that so easily entangles, and let me run with perseverance the race marked out for me. Forgive me. Heal me. Help me to bring my pain that hides within the crevices of my soul, those areas that remain in darkness afraid to be truly known, into the light of your presence. Let me fix my eyes on you, Jesus, the author and perfecter of my faith, who endured the cross, scorning its shame, and sat down at the right hand of the throne of God to be in relationship with me. Thank you that I am your joy and your delight. Let nothing hinder me from having an authentic relationship with you and with others. Wash me with your Living water and purify me of all sin. I confess you Jesus as Lord and rejoice in the knowledge that I am saved. Open my heart and my mind to learn through the following pages how to love the unlovable. In Jesus' name I pray. Amen.
Hebrews 12:1-3; 1 John 1:7-9; Romans 10:9.

GOD'S TRANSFORMING TRUTH
Walk with Jesus to have authentic relationships: "If we walk in the light, as He is in the light, we have fellowship with one another, and the blood of Jesus, His Son, purifies us from all sin" (1 John 1:7).

QUESTION TO PONDER
What are you ashamed of that restricts you from authentic relationships and prevents you from being the person God created you to be?

TAKE ACTION
Meet Jesus at the well of your heart. He sees you. He knows you. He hears you. Listen to His sweet gentle voice. He loves you. Make the decision to invite Him into your pain.

Chapter Two

Forgive to Be Set Free

Jesus said, 'If you forgive men when they sin against you, your heavenly Father will also forgive you.'
Matthew 6:14
'If you hold to my teaching, you are really my disciples. Then you will know the truth, and the truth will set you free.' John 8:31-32

Miserable, I thought: *Why did I marry this man?*

One day my husband announced his intended resignation from his management position at a computer software company. "Don't you think you should get another job before you quit this one?" I asked, already knowing the *right* answer and hoping I could change his mind.

What more could a man want? I wondered. After fourteen years of marriage Mark had a submissive wife, four children, a new five-bedroom home, and a management position at a growing company.

But Mark responded with anger, saying I was unsupportive and cared only about the money he made and not his well-being. For the first time in our marriage I opposed his decision and he felt disrespected. His response revealed the communication problems we had. Afraid of confrontation, I quickly agreed to support whatever decision he made, but inside I resented him and thought he was making a mistake.

Within weeks my husband quit his job, we were forced to rely on the vacation pay he had accrued and this only confirmed, in my mind, that I was right and he was wrong. Mark's intense personality made having him home 24 hours a day difficult. He was unhappy, and made it known. I was unhappy, but rarely said a word. Over the years I had learned to bury my feelings to the point of not being able to identify how I even felt. Deep down somewhere within the hidden memories of my past, fear of rejection held me captive.

Eighteen years passed before I slowed down to reflect on my youth. A book had been brewing within me for a couple years after a conversation I had with a random mom on the side of a community pool. While we watched our children take swim lessons we shared about our past. For the first time I exposed my secrets. She suggested I write a book, but I saw no point at the time. Not until I became a Christian did it make sense that my past pain had a purpose.

A couple days a week I snuck off to be alone with God to write. With Mark at home, he watched our two toddler boys, while our daughters were in elementary school. This began my 16-year journey to write this book. It took on many different shapes, beginning with letters to people in my life. Through the process, I learned a great deal about myself and my relationships. I remembered the pain of rejection that led me down a path of destruction. These letters became a tool to forgive.

Forgiving My Mother

After seeking God in prayer, with pen and pad, I wrote the letter to my mother. Recalling the conversation we had just days before my boyfriend, Eddie, broke up with me. My mother had suggested that I go on birth control pills. Stunned, I told her I was waiting until marriage to have sex. I heard the message of purity in my church youth group. But my mother dismissed my proclamation to stay pure. Instead of telling me to honor myself, the message I received was to have safe sex. Thinking back to a few nights later when my friend's older brother stole my virginity, I never screamed or fought or ran away. Curious about why, I realized that maybe I gave up too quickly. My mother had said that older guys would expect to have sex with me.

I cried out for God to reveal my pain and to release and purge every bitter memory that I carried in my heart. Years of hurt poured out on pages and pages of the letter I wrote to my mother. During the process of remembering, my mother and I had many wonderful conversations. Without accusing her, gently I asked about her experiences. She shared with me openly about her past. We shed many tears together mourning what we lost, and the decisions we made that impacted the direction of our lives. We embraced and empathized with one another as we bonded in ways we had never done before. The shame and darkness of our past was exposed to the light as we developed a truly authentic relationship. Restoration and healing began.

During the process of writing my lengthy letter to my mother, I remembered the details of my abortion. In a conversation with her about my abortion, she confessed her abortion. A secret she had buried for forty-five years. Her father said he would disown her if she ever became pregnant. Feeling like she had no choice, she aborted the baby. Prior to when abortion was legal, the man of the baby arranged the abortion with a doctor. Guilt and shame enveloped my mother over the years, knowing she had done something wrong but justified it. She hid behind a façade of trying to be perfect to obtain her self-worth through work and keeping busy, as I had done for many years.

Unintentionally, we disconnected from our children to survive the pain of the loss, to bury the memory, and to prove we could never be so bad as to take the life of our unborn children. Finally, I understood why my mother insisted I go on birth control at sixteen when I was dating an older man. At the time, I was unaware that my mother had become pregnant as a young woman. She projected herself upon me in fear that I too would become pregnant and be faced with an unplanned pregnancy.

My mother and I grieved the loss of our children, remembering every painful moment of that decision. We came to realize that our babies are in heaven. In a dream God revealed I had a little girl with long curly brown hair. I named her and wrote her a letter asking for forgiveness for taking her life, for causing her pain, and not giving her the opportunity to become the amazing person God intended. After mourning, I finally had peace knowing she was in the loving care of her heavenly Father. She had a new body with no more tears and no more suffering. I promised that one day I would hold her in my arms and kiss her tenderly.

Forgiving Josh

During the process of my healing, I wrote a letter to the man who raped me, although at the time I had never called it rape. Josh stole what was sacred; what was mine. His choice led me down a path of trying to win the approval of men in hopes of being accepted. His choice desensitized me to the importance of the holy union between man and woman designed by a holy God to be a beautiful act of love. Instead Josh perverted it to be an act of selfish gratification, to be used and tossed aside. I would go down a path of believing a lie that my purpose was to give myself away to gain approval.

At first, thinking about Josh made me angry, then I became sad for him. I wondered what his life was like now, whether he had a family and how he treated his wife and children. Was he lost? I realized I wanted him to know Jesus, and find love and acceptance through his Savior, not as a man who takes what's not his. I wanted him to value women as a special treasure from God to be cherished and adored like a delicate and beautiful butterfly. Fervently, I prayed for Josh to know his identity in Christ as a child of God and as a man of integrity. I realized as I wrote my letter to Josh that I wanted the best for him and I came to a place of total forgiveness.

Forgiving My Father

When I wrote my letter to my father I forgave him for not protecting me, for not treating me like his princess. He had rejected me. He had chosen work, women, and alcohol instead of his little girl and honoring his wife and keeping his family together. Even in his retirement years I sometimes felt abandoned by him. This one time, I discovered that his phone was disconnected, and then learned from my sister that he and his second wife had moved to New York City without telling me. When I finally reached him by phone and told him that I was hurt, he said, "Don't feel that way." Those words, *Don't feel that way,* pierced me. Is that why I had a problem expressing my feelings for so many years?

"Dad, I have every right to feel hurt and rejected. You left me without saying good-bye and without giving me the opportunity to visit you in Northern California before you left," I told him, "These are my feelings."

He agreed and apologized.

My dad can be one of the most charming men I know. He loves people. Everywhere he goes he makes friends. In many ways I take after my dad. He made it easy for me to love people and I love him for that. I realize that he is always going to be focused on what's in front of him, which is usually his political talk shows, his wife, and his dog. However, when I'm with him, he can make me feel as though I'm the only one who matters. When we're apart, months can go by until I finally call him. We can talk as though we just spoke a week ago. That's my dad and I have learned to accept him for who he is, because certainly I'm not going to change him. I can change me and choose to call him more frequently. In fact, in the life-transforming book *Boundaries,* Dr. Cloud and Dr. Townsend teach that you cannot change other people. However, you have the power to change yourself, if you see yourself as the problem. When you see someone else as the problem you give them power to control you. The problem with feeling controlled and powerless is that it will lead to blaming and bitterness.[2]

Through the process of writing my letters my perspective began to change from blaming others for my pain to trying to understand the pain of others. My curiosity peaked about my father's childhood. Over the phone we talked about his parents and his upbringing. I gained understanding of what molded and shaped him, and I felt compassion for him instead of judgment. His mother had rejected him through infidelity—a sin passed down through the generations. My Nana Ola was rejected by her father as a young girl when he left her family to move across the country to marry another woman. I saw the patterns and similar cycles of sin repeat from one generation to another. Dr. Cloud and Dr. Townsend also share in their book that we stay stuck in our dysfunctional ways when we refuse to forgive and expect the person who hurt us to make amends.[3]

In other words, there is nothing our family, or for that matter anyone else who injured us, can do to atone for the horrific atrocity committed against some of us. This is precisely why Jesus came to pay the price of that offense, that's why He was brutally beaten, mocked, betrayed, and hung on a cross. He died for the pain inflicted on us by others and the pain we inflicted on others and ourselves. Our pain allows us to draw ever so near to God. Mother Teresa explains it this way, "Suffering, pain, sorrow, humiliation, feelings of loneliness, are nothing but a sign that you have come so close to Jesus that He can kiss you."[4]

Remembering my pain, instead of blocking, I felt the loving arms of Jesus embrace me with His overwhelming comfort. By writing these letters I released my pain to discover that each of those painful memories molded and shaped me into who I am today – a child of God, a vessel He can use to relate to others. I love and adore my parents, and feel adored by them as we have healed our hurts. Although they made some poor choices, many of my good qualities came from them as well as some of the areas I needed to improve upon. And in that process of understanding who I was in relation to each of them, I looked at what sin had been passed down to me. God was asking me to examine my past choices, to make some decisions, and change the cycle.

Forgive to Be Right with God

Wounded, we attempt to soothe our pain through sex, drugs, alcohol, over-working, over-eating, over-spending, and exerting power over others. Along the way we hurt people as we continue to torture ourselves in search to numb the pain of betrayal. Only Jesus can satisfy our hearts' desire for the love we long for. He will heal our brokenness and help us to forgive and be forgiven. When we forgive we are blessed with forgiveness by our heavenly Father. The scripture promises, *"If you forgive men when they sin against you, your heavenly Father will also forgive you" (Matthew 6:14)*.

Forgiveness is not about the person who hurt you. We are instructed to forgive to be right with God. Our bitterness and hatred separates us from a holy and loving God. He forgives us, and He says we must forgive to be forgiven. You see, God knows that an unforgiving heart will cause us suffering. He wants us to be free of that pain, to have inner peace, and be in a right relationship with Him and the people in our lives. Forgive to be set free from the bondage of bitterness in order to love and be loved. Jesus said, *"If you hold to my teaching, you are really my disciples. Then you will know the truth, and the truth will set you free" (John 8:31-32).*

Do you know what Jesus teaches? That's the only way we can know the truth that will set us free. The truth is not a feeling. The truth is Jesus, the inspired Word of God, which will be taught in the chapter *Proclaim Your Power*. Until then just know that Jesus said, *"I am the way and the truth and the life. No one comes to the Father except through me"* (John 14:6). That's a bold statement. And we can conclude right now that either Jesus was a liar, a lunatic, or God in the flesh who was telling the truth. If you believe Him as the truth then you will follow Him and what He teaches, which makes you His disciple. When you are His disciple you will be set free from the bondage of sin that has you bogged down in bitterness toward people who hurt you.

Peter went to Jesus to ask how many times he must forgive, Jesus told him to forgive seventy times seven, which is four hundred and ninety times. The point Jesus was making in Matthew 18:21-22, was that we must keep forgiving as Christ keeps forgiving us.

Forgive to Accept Christ's Sacrifice

Accept Christ's sacrifice for your sin. We all make mistakes and bad choices that impact others, especially innocent children. Knowing that, we must stop beating ourselves up for the hurt we caused. Instead, humble yourself to ask for forgiveness. Go to those you hurt, take responsibility for the sins you committed against them, and do not make excuses for your behavior. Surrender yourself and your loved ones and all those that you hurt to God. Trust that God adores them and loves them and will answer your prayers for healing. Obey God when he says to forgive, and that includes accepting His sacrifice on your behalf. If you do not forgive yourself then you are saying that Christ's sacrifice was in vain and it was not good enough for you.

Even when our children are hurt by our choices and continue down a path of destruction we can pray for them and trust that God has them in the palm of His hand. He is faithful to our prayers and will bring purpose through the suffering. We may not see the purpose today, but cling to the hope of His promise that *"He works all things together for good to those who love Him and who are called according to His purpose" (Romans 8:28).* Sometimes it's hard to see the purpose through the pain. This was no exception for Bill who suffered with the constant reminder of his past choices.

Bill's Testimony

After awakening from a drunken stupor Bill found the note on the table from his wife along with her wedding ring. The note said something like, "Our marriage is over. I've packed my bags and I'm going to a friend's house." Distraught by the news, Bill noticed another letter sitting nearby. He began to read the horrible things he scribbled to his wife the night before when she had confessed her affair. Memories pierced him of how irate he had become and the names he had called her. In his drunkenness he had actually wrote on paper the words he had verbalized.

This was the breaking point for Bill, that he could be so cruel and abusive to his wife, after many years of neglecting her and their two children through his alcohol. With his nineteen-year-old daughter in rehab for drugs and alcohol addiction, he decided it was time for him to get the help he needed. After making arrangements to check himself into the Betty Ford Center, he called his daughter, Kimberly, at the rehab facility to tell her the news. Unavailable, he left a message with the staff for her to call him back. He hoped she would leave her treatment center to join him in Palm Springs to do rehab together. With all the plans made Bill decided to have one last drink at the local bar where he frequented often.

After returning home he listened to a message on the recorder from the director at the rehab facility. Kimberly had left treatment for no apparent reason. Someone from the facility dropped her off at the house to go home to her parents. Eager to see his daughter and share his news, Bill searched for Kimberly. First he looked upstairs in her bedroom. She wasn't there. He realized that she could be in the garage where she was allowed to smoke. Going through the door into the garage he saw her feet hanging at eye level. He looked up and saw his precious daughter starring down at him with the noose around her neck, a memory that would stay with him every day of his life from that moment on. He would be changed forever.

God used this event to completely humble Bill. He said to me, "The Betty Ford Center was the hospital. The chapel at the facility was the operating room where Jesus did surgery on my heart. Every morning I went into the chapel to cry out to God, to have him forgive me and deliver me of my addiction," he proclaimed, "and Jesus healed me."

After treatment Bill began attending AA meetings. He shared his story of how his destructive lifestyle of using alcohol impacted the lives of his family, how he had verbally abused his wife and lost her to infidelity, his daughter to alcohol and eventually suicide, and rightfully so, his son had been angry and bitter towards him.

A couple years later my mom married Bill when I was an adult, pregnant with my third child. He came into our lives professing his love for my mother, reassuring us children that he would not replace our biological father, but that he wanted to be part of our family. Within months I fell in love with Bill and asked him if I could call him Dad. Joy overwhelmed us as we realized that God had filled a void in both our lives. Our pain had come full circle and we saw that God had a plan through my distant relationship with my father and the loss of Kimberly.

Let me explain, God never wanted Kimberly to take her life. The stronghold of Satan kept her in the bondage of her addictions. The enemy whispered lies to keep her hostage to low self-worth, despair, and hopelessness. God, on the other hand, allowed her free will to follow Him or to follow the temptations of this world. Through her death, God used it to humble a man and heal him of his destructive lifestyle as well as restore and bless my family.

Although Bill was delivered of his addiction to alcohol, he held onto the pain that he caused his family, living with constant condemnation and guilt over his daughter's death. One evening when I was praying for Bill to be healed of his blood cancer, I sensed his hopelessness in my spirit and asked if he accepted Christ's sacrifice for Kimberly's death. With tears rolling down his cheeks he admitted that he couldn't forgive himself. Eighteen years had passed, yet everyday he thought about the image of Kimberly's face hanging from the rafters in the garage. That night Bill prayed that God would help him completely accept Christ's sacrifice for the pain he caused Kimberly, his son, and his ex-wife so that her death would not be in vain. We asked God to deliver Bill of bitterness towards himself. With a grateful heart we thanked God that He had worked Kimberly's death for the good and would continue to do so.

Several months later I asked Bill if I could share his story in this book. He was delighted with the possibility that his testimony could encourage someone to surrender their addictions to the foot of the cross to save the lives of their family. When I asked if he had forgiven himself, he said, "Oh yes, I surrendered completely to God and trust that He allowed Kimberly's death, maybe to save her from a life of destruction and more misery." I thought back to our prayer, God had healed my stepdad and had given him new life with purpose. Through the pain God had a plan. Bill has brought laughter, wisdom, and unity to our family. We adore him and cannot imagine life without him.

Steps to Forgive

1. **Invest in the process of forgiveness.** If you devote time to healing, you will reap a reward of peace and joy and the abundant life God has for you. To be set free from the bondage of bitterness that is holding you captive to destructive thoughts and behavior, you must expose your pain. For me, I used the letter writing process. You decide what is best for you. Think about the term "no pain, no

gain" used with physical activity when working out or training. An indication that you will gain muscle after a workout is when you experience the pain of sore muscles. Well, the same is true with emotional healing. You must go back to look at the offense, to remember, and experience the pain in order to heal completely and grow in maturity and godly character. It will come with tears that will cleanse your heart. Ask Jesus to reveal what you need to remember in order to heal. And ask Him to help you to forgive.

2. **Reflect on how that offense has impacted you.** To know what you are forgiving you must understand the damage done. Did the offense take you down a path of destruction? Certainly it caused bitterness and that has impacted your life. Bitterness is like poison. It hurts the one who drinks it, not usually the person you're bitter towards. In fact, the bitterness hidden within you will manifest as lashing out against innocent people. Also bitterness can keep you awake at night or in a depression or living in fear and anxiety or rehearsing the memory. As a temperature gauge measures heat, our memory of the offense will measure our bitterness. Forgiveness is not forgetting the offense, but when we truly forgive then God will gradually take those memories to make them less painful and eventually you will be able to minister to someone else who has experienced the same pain.

3. **Think about why the person hurt you.** Consider how the person who hurt you has been hurt. You are not excusing the behavior but having compassion for what they went through. Many are ignorant of the pain they inflict, because they are hurt themselves. There's a saying that *hurt people, hurt people*. Jesus taught that people are unaware of their actions. Jesus hung on the cross after being flogged thirty-nine times with a leather whip containing sharp metal pieces that tore His flesh to almost unrecognizable. A crown of thorns placed on His head, mocked by a jeering crowd, and nailed to a cross, Jesus cried out, *"Father, forgive them, for they know not what they do" (Luke 23:34)*. Jesus said to you and me, *you nailed me upon this cross, you have no idea what you did, and*

I still love you and forgive you. He asks you and me to do the same towards those who have caused us suffering.

4. **Decide to bless those who hurt you.** Of course, justice must be served if a crime is committed. Sometimes the biggest blessing we can offer is discipline and a consequence for the offense. But you are serving no purpose to seek revenge with your distain. Trust God to deal with the person. You don't need to make the person pay with jabs, insults, withdrawing, lashing out, gossip, or stewing over the incident. Your bitterness towards them is futile. You only hurt yourself. God promises to bless you when you bless those who do evil against you (1 Peter 3:9). This is discussed in more detail in the chapter *Overcome Evil with Blessing.* This does not mean for you to continue to allow someone to sin against you. God hates sin and wants you to have no part in promoting it. The following pages will guide you in the process to stop the behavior from continuing. Patterns of destructive behavior repeat until we bless the offender through forgiveness and prayer. By doing so, healing happens that breaks the cycle. That's why to forgive the people who hurt you is essential in order for you to promote healthy relationships within your family. Otherwise your pain is projected onto others.

5. **Think about the positive.** Especially if you're forgiving a parent or someone close to you, look for the good things you can point out in that person, the positive influence. Think back to a time to when this person was there for you emotionally, spiritually, or financially. It might be only one fun memory of somewhere you went, or something they bought you, or a family tradition, or a talent you acquired, or he/she supported you in sports or academics. Maybe the only good that came from that person is that you have more compassion for others who are suffering in a similar way.

6. **Choose to no longer be defined by the offense.** You are a new creation in Christ, healed for a purpose. You are no longer defined by labels such as: divorced, abused, stupid, unemployed, fired, rejected, raped. Instead, claim your identity in Christ, which is explained in further detail in the last chapter *Determine Your Identity.* God wants you to have an abundant life. You must forgive

those who hurt you for you to experience His peace and joy. After you pour your pain on paper then burn the letter. Symbolically, this will release your pain to God and prevent others from reading it.

If like me, you decide to bless the person you want to forgive, I suggest re-writing the letter from a place of healing. Begin with appreciation for what they were capable of giving you at the time. Confess your sin to take responsibility for anything you may have done to contribute. Express understanding of the pain they may have endured. Tell the truth of how that offense hurt you and let him/her know they are forgiven. Then tell a transforming truth from God's Word. If that person is still in your life, say what you want for the relationship with a solution. Here's an edited version of the letter I wrote to my deceased grandmother:

Dear Nana,
My father called to inform me of your death. For a moment I stopped working at my desk to listen. Would I go to your memorial service? My life was busy building my career, pregnant with my first child, buying my first home. I had no time to mourn your loss, a woman unknown to me. But today, ten years later, I wept the lost opportunity to know a lonely woman related to me. I mourned for my father whose selfish daughter was unavailable during his time of loss.

Growing up you never saw me. Peering through the glass case in your small living room I longed to play with your Barbie doll collection, but they were not to be touched. Each doll perfectly placed in their perfect outfit with their perfect figures in their perfect life: a reflection of your pain. The pain of your father's betrayal impacted you and me. The consequences of immorality caused emotional detachment and betrayal. The legacy of infidelity and divorce passed down to influence another generation; shaping me, my children, and theirs.

Nana, your frail body was just an outer shell of a hurting soul wounded from a past that no one will understand. Only God can fully know your suffering brought by the choices you and others made. My hope is that in your final days you understood the Father's love and the sacrifice of His Son that you might live in heaven with no more tears and no more pain. Grateful for the life brought through your son, I live today. You gave me the heritage of my faith, although it came with hypocrisy, I went back to church and found Jesus and I'm saved today.

Please forgive me for not reaching out to show you compassion when I had none to give. I love you and hope to see you someday in the glory of heaven where I can reach out to love the grandmother I never knew.

Through the process of writing letters I surrendered to God those people who rejected and hurt me. By being obedient to forgive I began to experience God personally. When you forgive, you will see Him at work in your life. Maybe not right away, but at some point you will look back to see God's hand in the situation, to see how He worked it out for good. This happened to Joseph when his brother's betrayed Him. Read more of his story in Genesis 37, 39-50.

Joseph's Testimony

Favored by his father, Joseph's eleven jealous brothers despised him. They sold Joseph into Egyptian slavery and faked his death to turn their father's attention toward them. Purchased by Potiphar, one of Pharaoh's officials, Joseph resisted the temptation of the devil and turned down the advances of Potiphar's wife, who then falsely accused Joseph of trying to sleep with her. He was sent to prison, but God showed him favor. The warden put him in the highest position over all the prisoners.

Joseph never became embittered or vengeful, but was humble. God gave him the ability to interpret Pharaoh's dreams that elevated Joseph to the second highest position in the kingdom. God granted him wisdom to save the people from famine and reunite Joseph with his eleven brothers and father. Joseph's brothers humbled themselves to their brother, asked for forgiveness and bowed down to him in fear, willing to be his servants. But Joseph said to them,

> *Don't be afraid. Am I in the place of God? You intended to harm me, but God intended it for good to accomplish what is now being done, the saving of many lives (Genesis 50:20).*

Joseph showed complete forgiveness knowing that God had a plan through the pain. God used the evil plot of the brothers to ultimately elevate Joseph to a position of authority in Egypt. He would be used to bring provision to the kingdom of Israel. Also, he brought salvation through Jesus by the lineage of Judah, one of the eleven brothers saved from starvation.

God loves you and He has a plan for your life. In your difficult circumstances He will lift you up with supernatural power as you humble yourself to forgive those who hurt you. Just as Joseph was promoted to a place of authority and honor, God will elevate you to a place of position to make a difference for His kingdom. Claim God's truth: *SURRENDER to God to be lifted up.* Read the following promise:

> *Submit yourselves to God. Resist the devil, and he will flee from you. Come near to God and he will come near to you. Wash your hands, you sinners, and purify your hearts you double-minded. Grieve, mourn, and wail. Change your laughter to mourning and your joy to gloom. Humble yourselves before the Lord, and he will lift you up (James 4:7-10).*

Surrender requires humility. At first glance this scripture in James may seem harsh. Nonetheless this promise from God has power. This scripture gives us hope! We can resist the devil and his strongholds when we submit to God. What an awesome promise. What an amazing God who would tell us how to conquer the evil of this world. You might say, "But this verse says God wants me to be miserable all the time." No. God wants you to recognize that you're a sinner. Often times we think of ourselves as better than we ought to. The truth is we need to be forgiven. We're double-minded, fluttering back and forth calling ourselves Christians but living with bitterness, pride, negative thoughts, fear, and unbelief in a mighty God.

This verse tells us to submit everything about ourselves to Him, sometimes moment by moment, and come near to our loving Father who has our back. When we do, someday we will be elevated to a place of ultimate glory with Jesus in heaven. Until then, when you humble yourself and repent you are lifted up out of the doom and gloom of your situation with resurrection power. Like Joseph, God will use the difficult people in your life to teach you, mold you, and then use you to be a messenger of His love and hope to save His people.

Not all people will take responsibility for their actions. They may never humble themselves, but we can still forgive them, pray for them, and show them grace as our Father in heaven shows us grace daily. We are only responsible for *our* actions by being obedient to what God tells us to do through His Word. And He tells us how to behave in the following verse:

Therefore, as God's chosen people, holy and dearly loved, clothe yourselves with compassion, kindness, humility, gentleness and patience. Bear with each other and forgive whatever grievances you may have against one another. Forgive as the Lord forgave you. And over all these virtues put on love, which binds them all together in perfect unity (Col. 3:12-14).

Once you understand how God has chosen you and shown you mercy then you will demonstrate that mercy to others. People who never repent from their ungodly ways, who refuse to forgive, will not produce the fruit of compassion, kindness, humility, gentleness, and patience. Instead their lives will reflect anger, impatience, and pride. God wants us to forgive as He has forgiven us and let go of the pain that prevents us from experiencing authentic relationships. Who do you need to forgive to experience the abundant life God has for you?

Our love for our Savior compels us to want to forgive. Overwhelmed with gratitude for the gift of salvation, we are motivated to follow and please Jesus. Choose to forgive. It may seem impossible, but God wouldn't tell us to forgive unless it was possible. We are empowered to forgive by the Holy Spirit that lives in us through a relationship with Jesus who rose from the dead. He promises that *"We can do all things through Christ who strengthens us" (Phil. 4:13 NKJV)*. Christ will strengthen you to forgive. When you do, you will be set free from the root of bitterness to truly love. Pray the following for each person until every remembered pain has been individually and specifically addressed out loud. In the process, consider writing the name of the person on a rock to throw into the depths of a body of water to symbolically remove the offense forever.

Forgiving Father, I praise your holy name. Thank you for sending Jesus to die in my place for all the sins that I committed against you, myself, and others. I submit to you and resist the devil and the temptation to hold onto bitterness and when I do you promise that the devil will flee from me. And when I come near to you, you come near to me. I grieve, mourn, and wail my double-mindedness of fear, pride, anger, and unbelief. I humble myself to you and praise you that I am lifted up with resurrection power through the Holy Spirit. Because you have chosen me as your holy and dearly loved child, I choose to forgive (name of person) for (name the specific offense) because it made me feel (alone, afraid, dirty, detached, desperate, hurt, rejected, unaccepted, unsafe, unloved, used, and unable to trust). Lord, I choose not to hold onto my grievances, but to clothe myself with compassion, kindness, humility, gentleness and patience. Bearing with others and forgiving whatever sins they may commit against me as you forgive me. Thank you that I can forgive through Christ who strengthens me and that I am set free from the bondage of my bitterness by your truth. What the enemy has meant for harm, you intend to use for good to accomplish what is now being done, the saving of many lives. I ask you to bless (name of person) with a spirit of revelation to the One true living God, so that Christ may dwell in his/her heart through faith, established in love to have the power to grasp how wide and long and high and deep the love of Christ, and to know this love that surpasses knowledge, and be filled to the measure of all the fullness of God. In Jesus' name I pray. Amen. James 4:7-10; Col. 3:12-14; Phil. 4:13; Genesis 50:20; Eph. 3:17-19.

GOD'S TRANSFORMING TRUTH
Forgive to be set free to love: Jesus said, "If you forgive men when they sin against you, your heavenly Father will also forgive you." "If you hold to my teaching, you are really my disciples. Then you will know the truth, and the truth will set you free" (Matthew 6:14, John 8:31-32).

QUESTION TO PONDER
Who do you need to forgive so that you may be set free from the bondage of bitterness to be filled with God's joy and peace?

TAKE ACTION
Pour out your heart in a letter using the Steps to Forgive without giving it to the person. Out of obedience confess your sin of bitterness and say a prayer to forgive each person to be set free to love.

Chapter Three

Teach by Example

He has committed to us the message of reconciliation.
We are therefore Christ's ambassadors, as though God
were making his appeal through us.
2 Corinthians 5:19-20

Mark chose not to work for over a year. I began to recognize patterns of behavior that we had established early on in our 14-year relationship. Our marriage was built on a foundation of deceit, disrespect, and the death of our unborn child. Unequal dynamics defined our relationship. In fact, it felt like I was still the student and he was the teacher. He led and I followed. Although he was only three years older than me, I had slipped into a pattern of allowing him to have authority over me instead of being an equal partner in the relationship. Longing for the protection and provision of a father, I had looked to him to meet all my needs.

Example of a Father's Love

Our earthly father plays a vital role in the way we love people, ourselves, and God. In fact, God designed a father to be a reflection of our heavenly Father. In the Bible Jesus refers to God as our Father by using the word Abba, which is the affectionate term we use for the word Daddy. God wants you to feel comfortable to run to Him as His precious child eager to nestle within the safety of His heavenly lap. In much the same way, we depend on our earthly father or daddy to protect and provide for our family. He works hard to meet the financial demands of our home and keep us out of harm's way. Children look to him for physical and emotional strength, to guard their hearts, minds, and bodies from the evil of this world. Our father should be a mentor, wise counselor, and spiritual leader in our home.

Boys want to view their father as their hero, and often they follow in his footsteps in the way he treats his wife, children, extended family, friends, and even strangers in the community. Daughters look to their father as their role model of whom they will marry. Women will often choose a man based on what is comfortable in their own father-daughter relationship or the relationship they witnessed between their mother and father. This is why a woman may marry an abusive husband when her own mother was abused.

Today in the United States millions of children are raised in homes without their biological father. Fathers may even appear to be physically present, yet emotionally they are unavailable through work, television, internet, compulsive activities, or addictions. Prisons are full of angry men and women abandoned or abused by their fathers, who themselves felt unloved and who acted out their pain toward others. Earthly fathers fail us. Many fathers are confused, wounded, and broken children who fight for acceptance, security, and a father's love into adulthood.

The truth is, deep within us all, there is a longing for a relationship with our heavenly Father. He created us to be in a relationship with Him. We try to fill that God-shaped void in our hearts with the temporary self-gratification of sex, drugs, alcohol, food, shopping, and work. The good news is that we are loved and adored by our heavenly Father. Answer the following questions to determine what you believe about your Father:

> ➢ Do you believe that God chose you over His Son, that Jesus paid the penalty of your rebellious heart and died in your place to bring you into His family?

> ➤ Do you believe that there is nothing you can do to win the approval of God, Jesus died for you while you were a sinner. His grace alone allows you to stand blameless in His sight?
> ➤ Do you believe that God takes delight in you and desires nothing more than an intimate personal relationship with you, His precious child?

If you believe these questions to be true, then you will act differently, you will treat people differently, you will show mercy and grace to others as it has been given to you by your loving Father from above. I'm not saying you won't have conflict. You will, but you will handle it differently than someone who is ignorant to the love of God. You will demonstrate Christ's love. And you can teach godly behavior to the unlovable by your example for the purpose to reconcile them to their heavenly Father.

My neighbor demonstrated Christ's reconciling love to me. When we started walking in the mornings, before I became a Christian, I noticed a peace about her, a joy in the way she delighted in God and His creation, and a love that radiated from her towards my children and me. In fact, at first I thought she was a little coo-coo in the way she marveled at God's creation on our early morning walks. Quickly, I discovered she had a personal relationship with Jesus. She knew the Father's love and she couldn't contain it.

God gives us His Spirit of love when we invite Jesus into our hearts. He wants us to behave differently, supernaturally empowered to love the unlovable by the Holy Spirit at work in us. He explains it this way in the scripture, *"To them God has chosen to make known among the Gentiles the glorious riches of this mystery, which is Christ in you, the hope of glory" (Col. 1:27)*. We represent Christ and His glory by the way we treat others. For Mel, his co-workers showed Him the love, acceptance, and peace of Jesus.

Mel's Testimony

In the employee lunchroom Mel observed Christians who studied the Bible and were filled with joy. One day a co-worker gently addressed the deep burden of pain and rage that Mel carried in his demeanor by simply asking, "Mel, do you know what Jesus said?"

Mel said, "No, what did Jesus say?"

His co-worker shared the scripture from Matthew 11:28, *"Jesus said, 'Come to me, all you who are weary and burdened, and I will give you rest.'"*

Those words resonated with Mel, giving him a desire to know more about *this* Jesus and to study the Bible during lunch with these men. Their consistent godly example ministered truth and love to Mel that he had never known before.

What Mel had known of his earthly father were the words, *"Get out of my house! If I ever see you again I will kill you!"* which had sent Mel running for refuge at the age of fourteen to a friend's house.

Three years before, Mel's wealthy and abusive father filed for divorce. He took revenge on his wife by declaring her an unfit mother in court and threatened the children if they did not choose to live with him. Winning custody he took Mel and nine siblings to the United States. Mel's heart broke when there was nothing he could do as a small boy to protect his mother and then at eleven years old when he left his mother behind on the island of Guam.

In San Diego, Mel's father remarried a woman with her own children, where Mel and his siblings were abandoned to the garage and experienced horrific abuse that resulted in broken bones. At fourteen years old, Mel spoke up against his father to protect his siblings. This was when his dad threatened his life with a baseball bat and kicked him out of the house.

Instead of allowing Mel to live with his friend's kind family, his outraged father gave custody to a relative with ulterior motives. As it turned out, Mel's uncle gave him drugs and molested him. With no one to turn to, Mel felt trapped. All the while, anger brewed inside. Until one day full of rage, Mel ended the abuse with a violent fight and sought refuge at another friend's house. To bury his pain he turned to drugs and alcohol that caused his hatred to pour out toward innocent victims.

Eventually, dealing drugs in a meth house, Mel met Latisha. At the time, she was dating one of the *Top Ten Most Wanted* criminals, yet Latisha had a desire for a better life, to get off the streets and stop dealing. Determined to change, Latisha became the catalyst for Mel to become educated in a trade that landed him a job at General Dynamics where he witnessed godly men who shared the love of Jesus.

Mel discovered he had a Father in heaven who adored him with an everlasting love and who promised never to leave him nor forsake him. Mel was adopted into God's family as he surrendered his life to follow Christ. With his new found faith, Mel decided he could blame his dad and stay angry or take responsibility and forgive him. Mel's abusive father told him, "You can blame me for a lot of things, but from *this* point on it's up to you how you want to live your life. You're old enough to know the difference between right and wrong." Once Mel accepted that truth and extended grace, his father became a Christian, as did other family members through witnessing Mel's life-change. Initially jealous of Mel's love for Jesus, Latisha began to notice her husband's changed behavior and emotions. Mel's godly example wooed Latisha to her Savior.

Because of their life experiences and knowing they were saved by God's grace, Latisha and Mel began to minister God's love to the incarcerated and their families. In the prison, Mel leads chapel service for the prisoners who will return to their families. When he shares his testimony of the horrific physical, emotional, and sexual abuse to these men Mel is overwhelmed by how many men relate to his pain. Some grieve their past to repent and surrender to their heavenly Father. Forgiven and cleansed, they become passionate for Jesus in the prison. Mel feels a sense of urgency to teach these men to get on the right track before they go home to their families. He gives a strong message to "man up" and to get ready for the real world that will crash down on them through temptation. From Mel's personal experience he emphasizes, "Unless you have the humility of Christ, you can't lead your family like you should." He desperately wants these men to treat their wives and children with honor and loving devotion to change the abusive patterns that continue from one generation to the other.

Mel's wife, Latisha, imagines what life would have been like to be a woman in prison or to have a husband in prison and try to raise her children on her own. This understanding motivated her to help women and children of the incarcerated. Latisha says, "The enemy is counting on the separation of the family to destroy the kids and perpetuate the evil through the generations. He starts with taking the father away and forcing the family to live in poverty and usually in low-income areas, exposing their children to awful things and potential predators. The enemy of this world looks for single moms, desperate moms or distracted aging grandparents to trust their kids to that one predator who seeks to destroy those children."

Latisha knows firsthand the work of the enemy, because she was sexually abused as a little girl. Although her grandparents and single mother loved and adored her and her mother worked hard to provide for all her needs, Latisha says, "It really does take the right community to raise children. Someone has to care and do something!" Latisha wants these women and children to know that she sees them and that they matter. When our heavenly Father asks, "Who can I send to be an example of Jesus," Mel and Latisha said, "Send us."

Example through Proper Behavior

Early on in my Christian walk I stood in the kitchen and yelled, "I'm not a moron!" I was frustrated that my husband was telling me how to put the dishes in the dishwasher the *right* way. He never said those words. But after years of burying my feelings, I did not want to be told what to do or how to do it. Mark responded in anger as well, raising his voice over mine, until our five-year-old daughter, Kylie, clung to me screaming at the top of her lungs, "S-T-O-P F-I-G-H-T-I-N-G!"

Suddenly, I saw myself as what my daughter saw…out of control, angry, and acting like a lunatic. What was I teaching my children by my behavior? Why did I lash out in defensiveness and anger? Bitterness had its stronghold on me. My lashing out in anger and short temper reflected unforgiveness. Through writing the letters, God was healing me, but at the same time it brought up a lot of junk that I needed to process. Eventually I did.

When I wrote my letter to Mark, for the first time I experienced feelings that I had buried. Although it was extremely difficult, I evaluated our past foundation and the choices I made regarding the abortion, moving in with him, selling my broken down car to become completely dependent on him, and keeping our elopement a secret for a year and a half. Naturally, remembering painful memories will cause us to evaluate our decisions and what we could have done differently. At the same time, we must recognize that not only did those choices cause us pain they also shaped us into the people we are today. In the midst of realizing we would do things differently back then if we knew what we know today, we recognize Christ has us exactly where He wants us in our journey with Him.

Instead of being angry at Mark for the early part of our marriage, I needed to take responsibility for what I allowed and the choices I made. Believing that he intentionally manipulated and controlled me during the time we were dating, and continued to control me, caused me to lash out in anger. Instead, I began to recognize that I allowed him to lead me at a time when I was desperate for a father figure to bring me safety, stability, and security. At that point in my life, I did the best I could and so did Mark with the tools that we had. Now I needed to establish a healthy way of expressing myself. I could respond differently. Why should it matter if Mark wanted the dishes loaded a certain way? It certainly wasn't any more work to load the dishes his way. I could have asked calmly for clarification, "Is there a reason it's better to load them your way?"

The truth is that this situation was unnecessary to argue about. I'm not saying to keep quiet and stew about it. That behavior is what brews bitterness inside and can later cause us to lash out in anger or become sick with disease. What was important was how I behaved as an example of Christ to my husband and my children, to my little girl who screamed at the top of her lungs for us to quit fighting. That's what mattered. When I look back on my behavior that's what breaks my heart; that my daughter saw a monster instead of a loving mother. God says we must,

> *Be imitators of God, therefore, as dearly loved children and live a life of love, just as Christ loved us and gave himself up for us as a fragrant offering and sacrifice to God. But among you there must not be even a hint of sexual immorality, or of any kind of impurity, or of greed, because these are improper for God's holy people (Ephesians 5:1-3).*

The word Christian means *"little Christ"* and *"Christ follower."* We should imitate Jesus. Each situation is a teachable moment to the people in our lives. We may be their only role model on how to love, to be kind and compassionate, and to communicate effectively. People are learning from us. This is probably why many people want nothing to do with Christianity. People like me have not always been the proper role model to those watching.

Reflecting back to when I walked with my friend, if I had seen Pamela yell as I did, I may not be a Christian today. I constantly have to evaluate my behavior. What I say and do teaches those around me. How do you want people to behave? Your kids will follow in your footsteps. I hate the saying, "Do as I say, not as I do." Of course, our kids will do what we do. If we don't want our kids to be disrespectful, to participate in sexual promiscuity, to lie, do drugs, smoke, and drink then we must clean up our act. We need to stop arguing and criticizing, lusting after things and people, and medicating to cope with life. If it's a problem to maintain a godly example then we need to seek God and His people for help. God warns us to not cause anyone to stumble. And as Christians we have a ministry to reconcile people to Christ. God says,

> *We put no stumbling block in anyone's path, so that our ministry will not be discredited. Rather, as servants of God we commend ourselves in every way: in great endurance; in troubles, hardships and distresses (2 Cor. 6:3-4).*

Example through Perseverance

We will suffer in this world through hardships and difficult relationships, yet we are called to endure the hardships for the sake of our ministry. If we know Jesus as our Savior then we have a ministry of reconciliation. Our intimate relationship with Jesus should propel us to want others to have the same hope we have. That hope is evident as we demonstrate an overwhelming peace and joy in the midst of our trial with the unlovable, knowing God is in control. He will work our hardship for the good as we follow Him. By persevering in love, we receive a reward. Through perseverance our character is built. Here's what God says,

> *Consider it pure joy, my brothers and sisters, whenever you face trials of many kinds, because you know that the testing of your faith produces perseverance. Let perseverance finish its work so that you may be mature and complete, not lacking anything (James 1:2-4).*

Our reward for perseverance and patience or long suffering is that we become more intimately connected to Jesus. We mature and are transformed into His image. Not by having a *poor me* attitude, but seeking to have an eternal perspective. Our eternal reward is to be in His presence in heaven filled with awe and glory. In the meantime, we can experience Him here in the everyday circumstances of dealing with difficult people as we endure our cross. There will be suffering as Christ suffered. The Bible is clear to tell us that to follow Christ we will suffer. *"To this you were called, because Christ suffered for you, leaving you an example that you should follow in his steps" (1 Peter 2:21).*

The truth is we will suffer for our faith if we are truly speaking out for Christ. This world hates Jesus. When you stand up to proclaim your love for Him people will hate you. This is why it's important to love them. Evil and darkness do not like the light, but the light will eventually invade the dark. We are to be Christ-like in the way we respond to situations and the people in our homes, at the office, in our schools, driving on the freeway, in the line at the grocery store, or wherever God takes us. Unless we model godly behavior with compassion and humility, no one will see the life transforming power of Jesus through us and desire a relationship with Him. Teach by example to demonstrate proper behavior that will allow God to make His love known through you. Are you allowing God to use you to be His reflection? Jesus said,

> *A new command I give you: Love one another. As I have loved you, so you must love one another. By this all men will know that you are my disciples, if you love one another (John 13:34-35).*

Notice that Jesus didn't say that only *some* people will know that we are his disciples. No, he says *all* will know we follow Jesus. Are you an example of Christ to *all* men, women, and children? Clearly God tells us to love everyone, not just a select few. What does that love look like? Here's God's definition:

> *Love is patient, love is kind. It does not envy, it does not boast, it is not proud. It is not rude, it is not self-seeking, it is not easily angered, it keeps no record of wrongs. Love does not delight in evil but rejoices with the truth. It always protects, always trusts, always hopes, always perseveres. Love never fails (1 Cor. 13:4-8).*

This extensive list of how to love is not easily achieved and we all fall short of this definition, because we're imperfect. Nevertheless God loves us perfectly in this way. The Bible uses several Greek words for "love" but God's perfect love is set apart by the Greek word "agape." Agape is His unconditional love for us. He gives us clear direction on how to love through this definition. This definition is not how we are to feel, but how to demonstrate love through action. This agape love, unconditional love that God demonstrates toward us, is an example for us to follow. When we are challenged to express God's definition of love, then we have an opportunity to pray and ask God to enable us to love in His strength and power, and not our own.

Make it your goal to be a reflection of Christ with those difficult and unlovable people. If the person is physically abusive, I address this issue in the chapter *Establish the Goal to Protect*. Otherwise, since Christ is compassionate toward you, so you can choose to be compassionate with others. Humble yourself and demonstrate self-control toward others in an attempt to reconcile them to God as an *"ambassador for Christ, as though God were making his appeal through you" (2 Cor. 5:18-20)*. Of course, you may stumble at times. God shows you grace just as you should show others grace when they stumble. You have the power of the Holy Spirit when you stop to invite Him into the circumstance. Although you may not want to humble yourself, God can change your heart. He changed mine.

Example through Humble Service

One day the doorbell rang as my dogs barked wildly. I greeted my neighbor who stood with his hands on his hips at the front door. I sensed his frustration. We had been through this before. Shaking his head he said, "I have poop on my lawn again. One of your dogs must have gotten out."

I turned to my young boys who were standing behind me and asked, "Did the dogs get out?" Both my boys shook their heads and insisted that the poop was not ours.

My neighbor argued, "You don't know. Your dogs could have gotten out."

Defensive I proclaimed, "My boys said the dogs didn't get out." My heart was pounding, but this time a still small voice said to me, *Clean up the poop.*

Once again my neighbor said, "I'm sure it's your dog. The poop looks the same as before."

I heard the words again *Clean up the poop.* I turned to one of my boys standing behind me defending our dogs, "Honey, can you go get a plastic bag?"

Frustrated that I was caving in to the neighbor, my son shook his head defiantly. I insisted firmly. My son returned with the plastic bag, complaining, "Mom, I know it's not our poop."

I assured my son that it was okay and I turned to my neighbor and said calmly, "I understand that you must be frustrated that dogs are pooping on your lawn and I'm sorry." I smiled with a joy that only God could give me, "I'm not sure if it's our poop, but I'm happy to clean it up."

We walked across the street engaging in small talk. I remembered that I may be the only example of Jesus he sees. He knew I was a Christian; he had come to me for prayers when his father was sick several years before. Now, I had the opportunity to demonstrate humility and pick up the dog poop. When I did it with the right attitude, I was filled with joy.

The next day, my neighbor said he saw the dog that pooped on his lawn and he apologized for accusing my dogs. I smiled, shrugged my shoulders and chuckled, "It's alright. I really didn't mind."

As a follower of Jesus, when we choose to humble ourselves, God is blessed and glorified. Think about how Jesus humbled Himself to wash the grimy feet of His disciples. I don't know about you, but I have an aversion to feet, especially dirty feet. Jesus said we are to follow His example and serve one another. I want to say to Him, *I'll do anything but feet*. Yet I know that when I say, *"anything but that,"* then my heart will be tested in *"that"* one area. So, it's better for me to surrender to however He wants to use me, even if it means dog poop or dirty feet. When I do, I will be blessed. Here's His promise:

> *Now that I, your Lord and Teacher, have washed your feet, you also should wash one another's feet. I have set you an example that you should do as I have done for you. I tell you the truth, no servant is greater than his master, nor is a messenger greater than the one who sent him. Now that you know these things, you will be blessed if you do them (John 13:12-17).*

God promises that we are blessed when we humble ourselves to serve. Sometimes service comes in the form of doing something that we don't want to do. Think of Jesus' example day in and day out as he served the multitudes of people who constantly surrounded him with their problems. Jesus stopped to listen, expressed compassion, and took action. Often the action came in the form of serving ungrateful people. Those people, like Judas, would betray Jesus and have Him killed, just like we did. Not only did Jesus serve, but He often went off to pray.

Example through Prayer

During the year that my husband was unemployed our communication problems intensified, and so did my resentment. But before God provided a job for my husband, God first needed to change my heart. I had to learn how to trust God with my husband, our finances, and every aspect of my life. This was a test of whether I believed God loved me.

At my Bible study I asked the women to pray that Mark would find a position quickly. I wanted him out of the house!

My wise friend, Pamela, gently rebuked me, "More importantly, we need to pray for Mark's salvation."

Stunned by her rebuke, I pondered her comment and realized she was right. As a new Christian I learned that my husband's acceptance of Jesus as his Savior was more important than a job. We needed to be one or what is referred to in the Bible as "equally yoked," which was growing in our faith and love for Jesus and having my husband as the spiritual leader of our family.

Soon after Mark quit his job I asked him if we could go on a marriage retreat. Mark was outraged that I wanted to spend money while he was unemployed, but God heard the cry of my heart. As it happened, circumstances allowed for Mark and me to go on our first marriage retreat over Valentine's Day weekend, all expenses paid. I knew it was God, who even provided childcare for our four children under the age of seven!

That weekend God opened my eyes to the enormous problems we had. Let's put it this way, I was unhealthy. I realized it on the first day when I was unable to express a single feeling when we were asked to identify three.

After we left the retreat, Mark's heart had softened. At home he suggested we pray together in my closet, since he had watched me faithfully go into my closet to pray every morning before my walk with Pamela. Mark witnessed my faithful prayers, indicated by his comment, "Let's pray in your closet, since it seems to be working."

Two weeks later God answered another prayer. Mark attended a men's retreat where God pursued my analytical husband to reveal truth to him. He came home a different man, filled with the Spirit of God. I felt adored and cherished and important for the first time in a long time. He focused on me instead of the children. He even told the kids, "Go play while I spend time with Mommy." To see my analytical husband share enthusiastically about the freedom he felt, as he surrendered his life to Jesus, gave me hope for the months to come.

My expectations were high. I thought God had instantaneously changed my husband. For two weeks we were in la-la-land until life happened and our expectations weren't met. God needed to replace the wrong foundation that we had built our marriage upon. God woke me up to become more aware of my feelings that I had buried and to start expressing them for the first time. Daily, I would have to surrender to God in the midst of conflict, trust that God loved me as I learned to communicate honestly instead of pulling away. God wanted me to seek Him and when I did He built my faith.

Get on your knees to pray, go into your closet or your car or a sacred place in your home where you cry out to God. Make this your altar where you sacrifice your time to worship God and seek Him with all of your heart. God will meet you there when you do. He promises,

> For I know the plans I have for you," declares the Lord, "plans to prosper you and not to harm you, plans to give you hope and a future. Then you will call upon me and come and pray to me, and I will listen to you. You will seek me and find me when you seek me with all your heart (Jeremiah 29:11-13).

God wants to bless you and prosper you with an abundant life filled with His peace, joy, and love. As you pray for the difficult person you will see God perform miracles. Pray to be the miracle. Pray that people would see Jesus in you.

Prayer is not an option. If you want a relationship with God you must pray. When you do, you will see Him at work. Answered prayer builds your faith. God calls you to pray for those who are unjust, who persecute you for your faith, mock you, talk behind your back, shun you, and verbally attack you. Pray for these people. You may be the *only one* on the planet praying for him or her. In Matthew 5:44-45 God says, *"But I tell you: Love your enemies and pray for those who persecute you, that you may be sons and daughters of your Father in heaven."* That difficult, nasty, and unlovable person needs you! Actually, that person needs God and God wants to work through you. Although that person may seem impossible to love, God has called you for the task and He knows you can handle it through prayer.

Whatever your pain, your circumstance, or difficult person you are dealing with, trust that God has not forgotten you. You may be reading this at work, at home, in a coffee shop, or in a prison. Wherever you are, God is with you and He loves you. He hears the cry of your heart as you humbly go before Him. While you pray, be patient as God works in your heart and in the heart of the person you are praying for. He is at work, even when you don't see the person changing or things get worse. Take heart. Know that God is faithful to His promises.

Be direct with God, don't beat around the bush or be general, but ask specifically. We must approach the throne of God as we would a loving father that wants to give us the desires of our heart. And then expect Him to answer. The answer could be no or to wait, but eagerly expect yes. And if *no* comes then know that God has a plan through the no. But let me warn you to not give up or you will miss the blessing that comes on the other side of the pain. Pray believing God is capable and willing to do all things according to His good and perfect will.

God can do a miracle as He did in Acts 12:5-16, when a group of Christians were praying for Peter. He was bound by chains between two soldiers that were asleep when an angel appeared in the cell. The angel woke Peter up and removed the chains from his wrists. Peter followed the angel out of the prison, passed the guards, and out the iron-gate leading to the city. The angel left and Peter went to the house of Mary the mother of John where many people were praying for his release.

The story goes on to say that they were astonished when their prayers were answered. How many times have you prayed without expecting God to answer? When He does you're shocked and amazed. Although your faith is little, God is faithful. The scripture says we only need the faith the size of a mustard seed to accomplish great things. In Matthew 17:20 the disciples asked why they failed to drive out a demon from a boy. Jesus replied, *"Because you have so little faith. I tell you the truth, if you have faith as small as a mustard seed, you can say to this mountain, 'Move from here to there' and it will move. Nothing will be impossible for you. "* This small seed is known for its rapid growth into a large plant. With our small faith we pray. God answers and our faith is built rapidly just like the mustard plant. God does miracles. Believe that nothing is impossible with God. He can do a miracle in your difficult relationship. He will move the mountains in your life as you are obedient to stay *"joyful in hope, patient in affliction, and faithful prayer" (Romans 12:12)*.

Time and time again I have seen God's faithfulness, miracles, and transforming power take place in the lives of His people when they seek Him in community. In the Old Testament the battle was won when Moses held up his hands in Exodus 17:10-12. He had the help of Aaron and Hur who stood by him, holding up Moses hands when he felt weak. Together they petitioned God for Joshua and the army who fought the battle against evil. This illustrates the importance of community standing alongside us in prayer in the midst of our battle. God has created the church body to intercede for one another. Through the remaining pages you will witness God at work through the faithful prayers of His people.

Pray in community to glorify God. Someone once said about marriage, "Those who pray together stay together." I believe God can restore any relationship if two people can come together in humility before God to *"confess your sins to each other and pray for each other so that you may be healed. The prayer of a righteous man is powerful and effective" (James 5:16).* If your difficult person refuses to pray with you, then at the very minimum, ask them how you can pray for him. Go one step further to ask them to pray for you. The blessing of coming together in prayer is that we hear the longing of one another's heart and healing can happen.

Petitioning God together in community is powerful. We experience God. Jesus said, *"I tell you that if two of you on earth agree about anything you ask for, it will be done for you by my Father in heaven. Where two or three come together in my name, there am I with them"* *(Matthew 18:19-20).* God is with you when you pray alone and He hears your prayers. However corporate prayer unites the body of Christ. In one Spirit God is petitioned with eager expectation of what He will do. The Spirit of God moves in a mighty way in the hearts of His people and lives are changed. People are healed and God is glorified through many people. Corporate prayer has prompted past revivals that have changed nations. God used Paul during a time of intense persecution to tell you and me how to pray, who to pray for, and why we should pray through the following verse:

> *I urge, then, first of all, that petitions, prayers, intercession, and thanksgiving be made for all people—for kings and all those in authority, that we may live peaceful and quiet lives in all godliness and holiness. This is good, and pleases God our Savior, who wants all people to be saved and to come to a knowledge of the truth…Therefore I want the men (and women) everywhere to pray, lifting up holy hands without anger or disputing (1 Timothy 2:1-4, 8).*

At the time, the Roman emperor, Nero, persecuted the church with harshness and cruelty. Nevertheless God encouraged the church through the apostle Paul to live peacefully under the rule and authority of Nero by submitting to his laws, praying together against evil, and praying for salvation for all people. Together we can make a difference in this world by our example of the Father's love, by proper behavior, through perseverance to serve those who are challenging, and to pray for them. Are you reconciling people to God by your example? Join me in praying:

I praise you Father God that you chose me to be your ambassador, to make known your love through Christ in me, the hope of glory. Equip me to love as Christ loved me and gave Himself up for me as a sacrifice to you God. Cleanse me of my sin of _____ and all immorality, for these are improper for your holy people. Help me to consider my situation as pure joy as I face this trial, because I know that the testing of my faith produces perseverance so that I may be mature and complete, not lacking anything. Let me put no stumbling block in anyone's path, so that I will not discredit my ministry. Empower me by the Holy Spirit to be patient and kind, not envious, proud or rude or selfish so that all men will know that I am your disciple. As I stay joyful in hope, patient in affliction, and faithful in prayer, I can move the mountain of (disrespect, bitterness, anger, negativity, complaining, overspending, lust of the flesh, and pride) because I have faith in you that nothing will be impossible for me. I humble myself to serve _____ by your power in me. I pray he/she sees Jesus in me and desires to know you, and to live peacefully in all godliness and holiness. In Jesus' name I pray. Amen.
2 Cor. 5:19-20; Col. 1:27; Eph. 5:1-3; James 1:2-4; 2 Cor. 6:3-4; 1 Cor. 13:4-8; Romans 12:12; Matthew 17:20; 1 Tim. 2:1-4, 8

GOD'S TRANSFORMING TRUTH
Teach by example to reconcile people to God: "He has committed to us the message of reconciliation. We are therefore Christ's ambassadors, as though God were making his appeal through us" (2 Cor. 5:19-20).

QUESTION TO PONDER
What are you teaching the unlovable by your behavior?

TAKE ACTION
Write a list of ways you can demonstrate proper behavior to those who are watching you.

Chapter Four

Motivated By a Pure Heart

Blessed are the pure in heart, for they will see God.
Matthew 5:8

Every moment of the day you have a choice to make. You can run from the conflict, or fight for righteousness, for truth, and for your family. Change can cause more conflict. It did in my marriage. More than I anticipated. There were many times I wanted to run away. Emotionally, I did. That was my story. That was comfortable for me.

Clearly, God told me to stay. Was it easy? Is it easy? No. Relationships aren't easy. Life isn't easy. But when we have God on our side, it's easier. He brings peace and strength in the midst of our storm.

We all have those challenging and difficult people in our lives, and sometimes, that unlovable person may just be you and me. Sometimes due to the choices we've made, we feel unlovable and undeserving of God's love and the love of others. In fact, not even aware we may sabotage relationships to prove we are unlovable. With that being the case, God loves us and wants more for our lives.

With only one month's mortgage payment left in the bank, God was testing my heart. What was my first love? Was it the material possessions that filled the rooms of my home or how much money I had in the bank? Was I willing to forsake everything for my relationship with Jesus? One night God woke me up to whisper in my ear through the still quiet voice of the Holy Spirit, *Are you willing to live in a tent?* In my quiet time with Him, I said, *"Yes."*

63

God wanted me to surrender everything to Him and to trust Him with my finances, my children, and my struggling marriage. Most importantly, beyond my comfort, was how many people would be in heaven with me. Saved people are the only treasures we take: our children, family, friends, neighbors, parents at the school, clerks in the stores, and maybe the homeless people at the shelter if that's where God would allow my family to go. I needed to get my priorities right to minister to whoever God wanted. I surrendered to the fact that it might be through losing my house. He might take me from the comfortable surroundings of my upper middle class neighborhood to share the gospel downtown. I knew that God was in control, not me, and I better be willing to give it all up for His glory; in whatever way He wanted to use me.

Looking back, many blessings came from the year my husband was unemployed. I learned to trust that God loves me, He knows what is best for me, and He will provide. I claimed the following promise that God was in control and He would show me the way to go as I trusted Him with every situation:

Trust in the Lord with all your heart and lean not on your own understanding; in all your ways acknowledge Him, and He will make your paths straight (Proverbs 3:5-6).

Mark had faithfully tithed to the church during the year he was unemployed. He realized that his previous employment and all his abilities, gifts, and talents had come from God. Mark had stayed home to read the Bible from front to back. He came across passages like Malachi 3:10, and had faith that God would honor His Old Testament promise that said,

'Bring the whole tithe (ten percent) into the storehouse, that there may be food in my house. Test me in this,' says the Lord Almighty, 'and see if I will not throw open the floodgates of heaven and pour out so much blessing that you will not have room enough for it.'

Mark was convicted that tithing was an area he needed to trust God with. As a new Christian, I had doubts that we should give money to the church without knowing how long my husband would be unemployed. At the time, I was unaware of God's promises about stepping out in faith to trust Him completely to reap His blessings. Nevertheless Mark trusted and followed God in this area. I watched my husband joyfully give each month from our retirement account, and my faith deepened as I saw God's faithfulness. Mark was finally ready to begin his job search. When he went to his knees in humility, he trusted that God would provide. God honored and blessed my husband with a job before the last of our resources were gone.

Finally, I came to understand our challenges with difficult people are all about our trust in God. In fact, there was a time that I resented Mark for taking that year off, for wasting our money, and him intruding on my time at home. I would take jabs at him when our finances were tight. One day Mark said to me, "Someday you'll thank me." He was right. I did eventually thank him for taking the year off when I realized that during that time I grew close to God, I spent time with Him in prayer as he took me on my journey to heal. I saw His faithfulness and I felt His love. *TRUST that God loves you.* Read God's promise:

For I am convinced that neither death nor life, neither angels nor demons, neither the present nor the future, nor any powers, neither height nor depth, nor anything else in all creation, will be able to separate us from the love of God that is in Christ Jesus our Lord (Romans 8:38-39).

God loves you. He died for you and nothing can separate you from His love. You need to trust that God is at work in your difficult relationship and circumstances. Do you believe that? You may not see the changes right away, but as you pray have confidence that God will bless you when you trust Him. Believe His promise, *"Blessed is the man who trusts in the Lord, whose confidence is in Him" (Jeremiah 17:7).* His blessings may come in the way that He changes you, draws you into a more intimate relationship with Him, and in the midst of your pain you experience His peace, joy, and comfort. The rest of this chapter will guide you to experience God more fully as you check your motives, attitude, thoughts, and the words that reflect the condition of your heart.

Check Your Motives

Are you motivated by a desire to glorify God or to glorify self; to protect or to punish; to encourage or tear down; to accept imperfect people like Jesus accepts us or to reject them; to serve others, including the unlovable, or to serve ourselves; to express our feelings in gentleness or to attack in defensiveness. Let your frustration level be a guide. Each time you want to lash out in anger or withdraw in despair stop to check your motives.

> ➤ Do you live in fear of what people might think, say, or do?
> ➤ Do you feel sorry for yourself and play victim by blaming and judging others?
> ➤ Do you have a spirit of unbelief that God can handle your problem?
> ➤ Do you lust after possessions, pleasure, or position?
> ➤ Do you live with a spirit of pride trying to prove you're powerful, perfect, and better than others?

Self-righteousness, self-pity, defensiveness, disrespect, greed, unbelief, and fear of man are all forms of pride. The enemy is out to destroy relationships, but the fact is *we* destroy relationships through pride. We cause quarrels by thinking we're right or smarter or justified or better than others. The Bible says in Proverbs 13:10, *"Pride only breeds quarrels, but wisdom is found in those who take advice."* Stop to listen to what the difficult person is saying and ask yourself, *what is God trying to tell me through this person? What advice do I need to take?* Ask God to show you if you are motivated by pride.

Jesus' half-brother James did not believe that his brother was the Messiah until after Jesus' death, resurrection, and ascension. Once James understood and believed that his brother Jesus was the Son of

God, he sacrificed all his selfish ambitions to preach the truth. From his own experience, God used James to boldly proclaim the reasons why we fight and quarrel in our relationships:

What causes fights and quarrels among you? Don't they come from your desires that battle within you? You want something but don't get it. You kill and covet, but you cannot have what you want. You quarrel and fight. You do not have, because you do not ask God. When you ask, you do not receive, because you ask with wrong motives, that you may spend what you get on your pleasures (James 4:1-3).

In this passage God tells us that our difficult relationships are motivated by selfish desires, which include bitterness, jealousy, greed, and lust. We argue and fight for what we want. Instead, we should be motivated by what honors God and what is best for the difficult person. God says,

Do nothing out of selfish ambition or vain conceit, but in humility consider others better than yourselves. Each of you should look not only to your own interests, but also to the interests of others (Phil. 2:3-4).

Remember, what is best for him does not always mean to give in to what he wants. The key is to seek God with a pure heart to know what is best. Trust that God will answer your prayers when you ask with proper motives for the purpose to reconcile that person to Christ. God may not answer your prayers for reconciliation until your motives are right.

Check Your Attitude

An attitude of gratitude will transform your relationships. By expressing appreciation we build people up. If we are not building others up then we may be tearing them down with our critical remarks. A critical spirit hurts people and destroys relationships. In fact, who

67

wants to be around negative people who criticize and complain? When we criticize, complain, and argue we push people away and disobey God, who says,

> *Do everything without complaining or arguing, so that you may become blameless and pure, children of God without fault in a crooked and depraved generation, in which you shine like stars in the universe (Phil. 2:14-15).*

Are you shining like a star for Jesus? Complaining and arguing are strongholds the enemy uses to destroy relationships, which ruins our testimony. A complaint often leads to bitterness that leads to gossip and eventually destruction. Have you ever been motivated by selfish desires that cause you to complain and nag and beg for your way? I have.

A few years after my husband was hired he was offered an opportunity to work on a project with his employer in Canada. During the year and a half we lived there we rented out our home. After moving back to San Diego I insisted that we change the flooring. After all, the renters had two cats. We also had raised our four children and two puppies with the same carpet and it was disgusting. My complaining and arguing to have new carpet and tile upset my husband. He wanted to wait until we could afford it. My bitterness pushed my husband further and further away from me. Feeling unappreciated and used he wasn't going to give me what I demanded. Looking back, I was acting like a spoiled brat. I just about destroyed our marriage with my attitude of entitlement as well as the disdain and disappointment I projected toward my husband.

Eventually, God gave me the new flooring. It wasn't until after I demonstrated a grateful attitude for what I had and patiently waited for what I wanted. It came down to whether I was willing to sacrifice material possessions for unity in my relationship. How quickly I forgot that this life isn't about the treasures of our temporary dwelling place on earth. In fact, I could have lost the house if my complaining continued to cause division in my marriage. In the end, God overwhelmed me with a grateful heart and filled me with more joy when I finally got what I wanted, but didn't get it right away.

Once more, let us encourage, exalt, and edify with words of appreciation. Instead of focusing on the negative and what we don't have, focus on the positive and what we do have and what people do right. Really, who wants to hear that we're lousy, lazy, and irresponsible failures? Those might not be the words we use but that's the message we convey by our tone of voice and nonverbal communication. Experts say that much of our communication is through body language. Have you felt like a fool by the expressions of someone? Maybe they rolled their eyes at you or shook their head in disbelief or disappointment. The truth is, quite aware of our failures, we already feel miserable. We already stand in condemnation of ourselves often before anyone has to say anything to us. Whether we let an inappropriate word slip from our tongue, we lose our temper and yell, stomp off in a tantrum, cut-off someone on the freeway, lose our job, over-spend or over-eat we recognize our weaknesses. We don't need to be beat down about them, but instead be encouraged to do better.

Clearly I remember the first time I made the conscious choice to respond to my husband without condemnation and disapproval. My behavior drastically impacted our marriage.

My husband had repeatedly explained the math homework to our son who was distracted. When Mark raised his voice in frustration to get Cameron's attention, I whispered, "Hey Mark, when you have a moment can I talk to you in the other room?"

A couple of minutes later my husband reluctantly followed me into the office. Behind closed doors I wrapped my arms around him and thanked him for helping our son with his homework. I expressed my gratitude for what he does for our family as an involved and dedicated father; a hard worker and great provider; and a committed and faithful spouse. My words of encouragement and acceptance melted his heart and changed his demeanor. He confessed to me that he thought he was in trouble. But instead, I accepted and appreciated him. I allowed him to be imperfect and encouraged him to be better by focusing on the good, which made him want to be better. He knew I believed in him.

Please don't misinterpret my illustration. I'm not suggesting that we allow improper behavior to continue without saying anything.

Instead, decide to accept one another as a work in progress, since God says to be confident, *"that He who began a good work in you will carry it on to completion" (Phil. 1:6)*. When you plan to discuss the areas of opportunity for growth, first let them know that we all have areas that we need to work on. First, build them up to build trust.

Our positive words of affirmation will build them up to desire to be a better person, to be eager to please, and later on to show *you* the same grace and acceptance in *your* weaknesses. A perfect illustration of this kind of acceptance is when Jesus demonstrated His love for us when we were still sinners. Each day He accepts us right where we are. He accepts our flaws and all our imperfections. His acceptance extended with outstretched arms on a wooden cross as He willingly died in our place when we were unlovable. He never expected us to be perfect before He accepted us. We are accepted fully and completely by His grace and mercy. When we come to that understanding we want to be better, we want to please Him.

To demonstrate our love for Jesus we live according to His ways by loving others. By extending unwarranted acceptance we show the unlovable person the love and acceptance of Jesus. When they experience that kind of love from us they are compelled to demonstrate their gratitude in ways that we can't imagine, but even if they don't, that's alright. We are motivated by a desire to change ourselves, not them. They eventually change, but it begins with us. Delight in difficult people! Build them up. Make it your challenge to point out her great qualities. You can do it! Focus on the positive NOT the negative. Give her hope through your words of affirmation. Follow God's Word when He tells you the following:

> *Do not let any unwholesome talk come out of your mouths, but only what is helpful for building others up according to their needs, that it may benefit those who listen (Ephesians 4:29).*

Did you read that? No harmful words should be uttered from your mouth. Yet there is a time to have a constructive conversation to discuss opportunities for growth that will be outlined in the chapter *Express Truth in Love*. In the meantime, remember to have an attitude of gratitude. Look at the contribution that person makes in your life even if you think it's minimal. Imagine life without them to determine the benefits they bring to the relationship. View your relational glass as half full not half empty or better yet, view it as full. To help you focus on the strengths of the difficult person in your life look at the following list of positive qualities and circle what applies:

Analytical	Forgiving	Motivated	Responsible
Artistic	Generous	Organized	Romantic
Committed	Gentle	Patient	Sensitive
Dedicated	Helpful	Perceptive	Supportive
Dependable	Honest	Persistent	Sincere
Encouraging	Humble	Positive	Strong
Expressive	Intelligent	Protective	Talented
Faithful	Kind-hearted	Reliable	Thoughtful
Flexible	Loyal	Respectful	Trustworthy

Circle the qualities you appreciate about your spouse; your children, and even your rebellious teenager; co-worker or boss; neighbor or friend; in-law, parent, or sibling. Once you have a list of positive qualities your goal is to focus only on the positive and fill in the blanks. If you're talking to your child or teenager your conversation may look like this:

"I want you to know that I think you're an amazing person. I'm proud of you. I see that you're committed and dedicated toward (school, sports, your hobby, friends, work, or the dog). You're thoughtful and loyal which will take you far in your future career and family. I know you'll be successful at whatever you choose to do."

If you're talking to a spouse or even an ex-spouse or an in-law, your conversation might look like this:

"Although I haven't expressed it much, I think you're an amazing person. You have made a difference in my life and our family. And I want to thank you for all the times over the years that you've been <u>helpful</u> and <u>encouraging</u> and <u>supportive</u>. I appreciate what you've contributed to our family. Those are things I once took for granted, but I want you to know that I'm grateful. I love you and I'm here to support you."

Changing your negative outlook can transform your relationship. Imagine if you started every conversation with the words, "You're amazing. I'm proud of you. I appreciate you for (<u>list all the positive qualities and what they do</u>)." Do it and watch what happens. Jesus preached a message on the attitudes we are to possess to be blessed.

How-to-Be-Blessed-Attitudes:
➢ Blessed are the poor in spirit (desperate for God, not seeking after earthly riches, influence, position, or honor), for theirs is the kingdom of heaven.
➢ Blessed are those who mourn (lament alongside others), for they will be comforted.
➢ Blessed are the meek (who display a gentle spirit that solely relies on God), for they will inherit the earth.
➢ Blessed are those who hunger and thirst for righteousness (who are obedient to God's Word), for they will be filled (with joy and peace).
➢ Blessed are the merciful, for they will be shown mercy.
➢ Blessed are the pure in heart, for they will see God.
➢ Blessed are the peacemakers, for they will be called children of God.
➢ Blessed are those who are persecuted because of righteousness, for theirs is the kingdom of heaven.
➢ Blessed are you when people insult you, persecute you and falsely say all kinds of evil against you because of me (faith in Jesus). Rejoice and be glad, because great is your reward in heaven, for in

the same way they persecuted the prophets who were before you (Matthew 5:3-12).

The Beatitudes have an eternal perspective. View this world and your life here on earth as temporary, only but a vapor in the scheme of eternity. Long for heaven and be motivated to bring heaven to earth by being the love of Jesus. Recognize that you are the vehicle to lead people to their heavenly home. The Beatitudes are God's promises that you are blessed when you stop thinking about yourself to think of others. Are you experiencing God's abundant blessings? Take the focus off of you. When you do, you will be less concerned about how your life is impacted by people and more focused on how you can impact people's lives. Discover true joy and happiness doing life God's way.

Check Your Thoughts

During conflict I often thought of the past. The more I played the negative tapes in my mind the more I resented my husband. I dug myself into a pit of despair. The enemy had a stronghold on my mind. I believed his lie. I believed that my marriage would never improve. Although I saw the hand of God in my life, I wanted out of my pain of hopelessness and struggles here on earth with my four young angry children and a husband who resented me during a time my son battled leukemia. My constant negative thoughts brewed hatred toward him.

During that time, I attended an Anne Graham-Lot's conference with over-the-counter sleeping pills stashed away in my purse. Feeling desperate and unloved, I remember when Anne looked at the audience and said something like, "Someone out there is in the pit of despair. You're feeling hopeless right now like you want to give up." Tears poured down my face as her words touched my pain. She went on to say something like, "Take your eyes off your problems and look up out of the pit. Take the hand of Jesus. He loves you. He wants to lift you out of the pit of your despair."

Alone in that auditorium with thousands of women God spoke to me. He was with me. He knew my pain. He saw me. Reaching into my pit Jesus extended His hand. I looked up and grabbed on. Slowly He lifted me out of my despair and put me on the firm foundation of His Word as I clung to His promises. Jesus said to me in His loving voice, *"For I am the Lord, your God, who takes hold of your right hand and says to you, Do not fear; I will help you" (Isaiah 41:13)*. That weekend the words, "Stop the pity party and start focusing on others" spoke to my heart. God revealed my sin of self-centeredness and unbelief in a powerful God who loves me.

Our thoughts have power over us. When we believe a lie we succumb to a stronghold from the enemy. Satan whispers lies in our ear that we play over and over. Examine the following list to recognize the lies you may believe:

➢ Nobody likes me. I'm too much to handle.
➢ I don't deserve to be treated better because of my past.
➢ I have to sacrifice this area of intimacy, since I'm damaged goods.
➢ I have to pretend to be perfect in order to be accepted.
➢ I will never change or conquer this sin.
➢ My relationship will never improve.
➢ He/she is a jerk and will never change.
➢ If I say what I think or feel or want, I will be rejected.
➢ If people really knew me they wouldn't accept me.

These thoughts are lies from Satan. Stop to recognize if negative thoughts are playing in your head. These negative thoughts may be about yourself or others. Are you listening to old messages that you heard as a child or from an abusive relationship? Do you dwell on negative circumstances from your past? Let me just say, Satan wants to keep you focused on the past, on the negative junk. Get rid of the garbage. The Deceiver wants to destroy and discourage you from having successful relationships. If he can use negative thoughts to cause dissension then he will be successful to destroy your family, future generations, and the unity of the church. Don't give him that power.

Our thoughts can lead to death and destruction. Believing wrong information can kill us. For example, if I believe a bottle of poison is apple juice, because that's what the label says, I will die when I drink it. Satan wants to deceive us by putting false labels on things that are dangerous. Our society is telling us lies. The ways of this world appear lovely, appetizing, and enjoyable like the delicious apple that poisoned Snow White or the forbidden fruit in the Garden of Eden. God warned Adam and Eve not to eat of the fruit just as He warns us today, but Satan constantly whispers false information to distort the reality of our choices.

We can easily justify our behavior with God's Word. We might say God wants me to be sexually intimate with my spouse, therefore, my wife should be available to me three times a day; or in the Bible men had concubines, therefore, I can have a mistress too; or Jesus drank wine, therefore, I can have my bottle of wine to relax every night. There are people who take scripture out of context to justify sinful behavior. Others expect everyone to live by the Law, because that's what they do, and when someone stumbles they show no compassion. Disguised as standing for righteousness, we destroy many of our relationships.

Well aware of the enemy's plans to deceive us, God provided a way to conquer the enemy. He demonstrates our key to success through Jesus who was tempted in every way by Satan in the desert after a forty day fast. Thankfully, in Matthew 4:1-11, we learn how to rebuke the enemy with the Word of God. Jesus was hungry and Satan came and said, *"If you are the Son of God, tell these stones to become bread." Jesus answered, "It is written: 'Man does not live on bread alone, but on every word that comes from the mouth of God.'"* The devil tempted Jesus again and He answered, *"It is also written: 'Do not put the Lord your God to the test.'"* A third time, the devil tempted Jesus with power and wealth and Jesus said to him, *"Away from me, Satan! For it is written: 'Worship the Lord your God, and serve Him only.'"* The devil was defeated by God's Word and angels responded by ministering to Jesus' needs. And the same is true for you.

So what does God tell us to do? We must know God's Word to rebuke the lies of the enemy. We must not let society mislead us with its alluring advertisements, tantalizing TV shows, and mesmerizing music. With negative messages come negative thoughts that enter into our minds to deceive and destroy us. Instead God says in Romans 12:2,

> *Do not conform any longer to the pattern of this world, but be transformed by the renewing of your mind. Then you will be able to test and approve what God's will is—his good, pleasing, and perfect will.*

Our thoughts dictate our actions, which impact the outcome of our relationships. Pride thinks we're better. Fear of rejection causes us to withhold love. Unbelief that God loves us will hold us captive to false thinking. God gives us His truth to conquer the lies of the enemy. The truth of God's Word will set us free. His promises will renew our mind and guide us into His perfect will for our relationships. To have victory over the enemy we must know the truth, believe the truth, and obey the truth of God's Word.

Our feelings are powerful. The emotions we have toward someone are felt regardless of how hard we try to put on the fake smile or sugar coat the situation. My husband and I learned to call it "residue" when we refer to the distance or barrier we feel in our relationship. After a disagreement we try to resolve the conflict quickly, but sometimes it takes time to process our feelings and understand what happened. If my husband senses that I'm still upset he will gently say, "Is there any residue from our disagreement that we need to talk about?" Or I might say, "I sense something is wrong, are you okay?" This gives us another opportunity to talk about the situation, to get clarity and understanding. We can forgive and move forward without any negative thoughts that will keep us distant or create a stronghold of bitterness.

For years I believed the lies of the enemy. When my husband would raise his voice I used to think negative thoughts like: *There he goes again. What a jerk. He'll never change. Why did I marry him?* If you find yourself playing negative tapes and messages in your mind, then stop! In the Bible we are taught to think on what is true. Look at the following passage,

> *Finally, brothers, whatever is true, whatever is noble, whatever is right, whatever is pure, whatever is lovely, whatever is admirable—if anything is excellent or praiseworthy—think about such things (Phil. 4:8).*

Change your thoughts to right thinking and what is true and praiseworthy, which are the promises of God. Focus on what God is doing and going to do in your difficult relationship. This will change your attitude toward the difficult person. Shifting your thoughts to one of praise will allow your motives and heart to become more pure. I can change those same negative thoughts mentioned previously to what is true about my husband. For example: *He's raising his voice. He must be frustrated. I wonder if he had a stressful day. He works so hard for our family to provide. He's dedicated and committed to our children and me. I know God is working on his heart. I'm glad that I married him so I can be here to pray and encourage him.*

Change the negative to a positive. Take the approach that something is hurting the person. Consider that he or she is feeling rejected or condemned. Changing your thoughts to what is right, true, pure, lovely, admirable, excellent, and praise-worthy you will see God at work. He allows the difficult situation as a test of your heart. When you hold your thoughts captive you can express empathy, gentleness, and patience toward the difficult person. When you do, they see the power of God. The enemy is conquered! You demolish strongholds. The scripture promises,

> *For the weapons of our warfare are not carnal but mighty in God for pulling down strongholds, casting down arguments and every high thing that exalts itself against the knowledge of God, bringing every thought into captivity to the obedience of Christ (2 Cor. 10:4-5 NKJV).*

Take every thought captive to think on God's truth. Eventually, you will stop listening to the negative tapes by reciting His positive promises. When you stumble into a pit of poor-me-I-deserve-better or she will never change then confess that sin with a broken and contrite heart, which God will honor, (Psalm 51:17). He does not want you to worry or doubt His power to convict a person of sin and change their heart. To do this may require you to do things differently.

To begin, it's important to stop wallowing in the pain of your relationship. Instead believe that God has a plan. Stop focusing on your problems and start focusing on your blessings. Stop being self-focused and start being other-focused. Not as a co-dependent trying to please others to get your self-worth, but to be used by God as a way to minister the love of Jesus. For me, as God would have it, a week after the Anne Graham-Lots conference a woman I had shared the gospel with asked if I could start a Bible study. God put several women into my life to focus on as we studied the Word of God together. Over time these women committed their lives to Christ. God took me out of the pit of self-pity to be filled with His joy on the firm foundation of His truth.

Check Your Heart

A stone heart is cold, insincere, insensitive, bitter, and selfish. A heart of flesh is moldable and teachable, gentle, soft, compassionate, and loving. Our physical heart is what pushes the blood through our body to sustain life. Without blood we have no life. We are physically dead. The same is true with our spiritual life. Jesus' blood gives life. Without it we are dead in our transgressions. Once we accept Jesus blood poured out for our sins then we have spiritual life.

The Holy Spirit gives spiritual life and resurrection power for us to have a pure heart. Ask God to reveal truth about your heart. Stop to listen to your words. That which comes out of your mouth is a reflection of your heart. Jesus said,

The good man brings good things out of the good stored up in his heart, and the evil man brings evil things out of the evil stored up in his heart. For out of the overflow of his heart his mouth speaks (Luke 6:45).

What words are you speaking? Are your words giving life or death? When your heart races with irritation or frustration ask yourself, *is my heart tender and loving, seeking the best for this person?* Be honest. Are you being selfish? If you are, then evil things are coming out of your heart. Selfishness, pride, bitterness, impatience, and fear come from succumbing to our fleshly desires and believing the deception of the enemy.

God blesses a pure heart motivated by unselfish desires, a grateful attitude, and thoughts that are based on God's truth. God promises, *"Blessed are the pure in heart, for they will see God" (Matthew 5:8).* If you want to see God at work in your life, including in your difficult relationship, then get right with God. The way to get right with God is to confess your sin. God promises that *"if you confess your sins He is faithful and just to forgive you and purify you of all unrighteousness" (1 John 1:9).* Did you catch that promise? You are purified, cleansed, and righteous when you confess your sins. Sometimes you have to confess moment by moment your negative thoughts. The quicker you confess your sinful thoughts the quicker God can heal and restore your broken relationships.

Each moment of the day is a test of your heart. God already knows your heart, but He tests you to reveal your heart to yourself and those watching. God says,

We speak as men approved by God to be entrusted with the gospel. We are not trying to please men but God, who tests our hearts (1 Thessalonians 2:4).

Did you grasp that promise? You are entrusted with God's transforming truth, with the message of salvation through Christ, and with the Holy Spirit that lives in you to please God.

Abraham's Testimony

Abraham had experienced God and seen His faithfulness by giving him a child in his old age. When God asked Abraham to sacrifice his teenage son, Abraham obeyed God even when it didn't make sense. Abraham completely trusted God's love for him and his precious child. In the same way, we demonstrate our heart through obedience. Abraham's words to his servants, who traveled with him to the place near where he would sacrifice his son, reflected the condition of his heart. He said to them, *"Stay here with the donkey while I and the boy go over there. We will worship and then we will come back to you."* Abraham trusted that God would do a miracle. As his son Isaac walked alongside his father, Isaac questioned where the sacrifice was for the offering. Abraham confidently replied, *"God Himself will provide the lamb for the burnt offering, my son" (Genesis 22:5, 8).* Abraham completely trusted God's promises and His provision. His desire to please God through unharnessed obedience was rewarded.

God stopped Abraham from taking the life of his son, but only after he had bound Isaac on the altar and lifted his knife to slay him. Can you imagine the complete trust that Isaac had for his father and for God to provide as he was bound on the altar? His faith was strengthened as God provided a sacrificial ram to be sacrificed in his place, which God later did for us through Jesus, who is called the Lamb of God. This was a test to show Abraham and Isaac that their heart was pure and holy before God. Isaac discovered how to completely love God by watching his father. Together, they heard the angel of the Lord say, *"Through your offspring all nations on earth will be blessed, because you have obeyed me" (Genesis 22:18). OBEY God to demonstrate your love and see Him at work.* Read God's transforming truth promised by Jesus,

> *Whoever has my commands and obeys them, he is the one who loves me. He who loves me will be loved by my Father, and I too will love him and show myself to him (John 14:21).*

Did you catch that? God shows Himself to you! When you follow the Word of God you will experience Him intimately at work in your life. As you obey you experience His power and strength in times of difficulty, His peace and joy in times of sorrow and hardship, and His provision and presence wherever you go. You will see Him at work and recognize Him in everything that happens moment by moment. Does this mean God does not love you when you disobey? Of course not! He loves you with an unfailing love. It was His love that wooed you to your Savior when you were rebellious, and it was His love that kept Him nailed on a cross to save you and me when we were still sinners. However, when we obey He gives us a deeper sense of His presence in our lives. We will *know* Him intimately and sense His delight in us. We will *know* His love. What greater joy is there than that?

Completely surrender to God's will. Lay down your marriage, your child, your parents, your career, and put nothing before your allegiance to God. Moment by moment, trust God with every situation knowing that it's a test of your heart. Discover in the next chapter how God will test your heart by giving you power. The question is will you use it? I was put to the test.

I praise you Father God that I can trust you with all of my heart and lean not on my own understanding as you make my paths straight. For I am convinced that neither death nor life, neither angels nor demons, neither the present nor the future will be able to separate me from the love of Christ. Forgive me for my selfish motives and pride. Help me do everything without complaining or arguing and let no unwholesome talk come out of my mouth, but only what is helpful for building others up according to their needs and benefit those who listen. Let my words be a reflection of a pure heart so that I may be blessed with your peace, presence, and joy. Help me not conform any longer to the pattern of this world, but be transformed by the renewing of my mind so I can test and approve your good, pleasing, and perfect will. Help me to think on what is true, noble, right, pure, lovely, admirable, excellent and praiseworthy. For the weapons of my warfare are mighty in you for pulling down strongholds, casting down arguments and every high thing that exalts itself against your truth. Help me bring every thought into captivity to the obedience of Christ. Empower me by your spirit to

obey your Word to demonstrate my love for you, experience your love, and see you at work around me. In Jesus' name I pray. Amen.
Prov. 3:5-6; Romans 8:38-39; James 4:1-3; Phil. 2:14-15; Eph. 4:29; Luke 6:45; Romans 12:2; Phil. 4:8; 2 Cor. 10:4-5NKJV; John 14:21

GOD'S TRANSFORMING TRUTH
Be motivated by a pure heart to see God: "Blessed are the pure in heart, for they will see God." (Matthew 5:8)

QUESTION TO PONDER
What are the negative thoughts rehearsing in your mind?

TAKE ACTION
Confess your negative thoughts to God. With an attitude of gratitude make a list of all the positive qualities in your difficult person and make a point to speak words of appreciation.

Chapter Five

Proclaim Your Power

*For God has not given us a spirit of fear, but of power
and of love and of a sound mind.*
2 Timothy 1:7NKJV

We had survived a year without income or medical insurance when my husband returned to the workplace as an engineer. Seven months later, I experienced God's power when our five year old son, Connor, was diagnosed with a rare form of leukemia (AML). During this tumultuous time, I claimed the power of God through His promise in Phil. 4:13, *"I can do all things through Christ who strengthens me."* In that verse Paul refers to the ability to endure hardships, persevere, and be content in all circumstances.

I would need God's strength to endure.

At the time of Connor's diagnosis, Mark and I could barely tolerate one another. Emotionally separated and alone, God said to me in His still small voice, during Connor's one hundred days of isolation, *"My grace is sufficient for you, for my power is made perfect in weakness"* (2 Cor. 12:9).

God's promise gave me comfort in my time of struggle. I came to fully understand what that scripture meant. I learned to completely rely on God for my strength and not on my own power or understanding. I was broken and lonely during a time when I needed my husband and he needed me, but we didn't know how to be there for one another. The remainder of the scripture that the apostle Paul wrote from prison says,

Therefore I will boast all the more gladly about my weaknesses, so that Christ's power may rest on me. That is why, for Christ's sake, I delight in weaknesses, in insults, in hardships, in persecutions, in difficulties. For when I am weak, then I am strong (2 Cor. 12:9-10).

God gave both my husband and me the strength to endure the hardships of a great deal of stress during our son's battle with leukemia and the very real possibility that he might die. The doctors said Connor had less than a fifty percent chance of survival with a bone marrow transplant, but I announced boldly to family and friends, "My God doesn't work in percentages." God prepared me for such a time as this. He had built my faith. He would sustain me whether in life or death.

Power of Surrender

Surrender yourself to God's plan and purpose. Relinquish control. The sooner we realize we are not in control the better. God is in control. He is sovereign over all creation and allows each circumstance for a purpose. Surrender is to get out of God's way so He can deal with the difficult person that we're trying to control in our subtle ways. Surrender requires humility and letting go of our pride that says we can fix it on our own. Surrender is not giving up on the person or the relationship or the difficult circumstance, but instead it's looking up to God and saying, *"I need you. You alone are worthy of my devotion, no matter what my circumstance. Help me to see this from your perspective. Use me for your glory."* Surrender is about your devotion to God Himself and nothing else.

Look to Jesus as your example of surrender. True surrender brings glory to God and an abundant life here and into eternity, not just for your gain but also for the benefit of others. Jesus surrendered unto death to bring you life. In the garden of Gethsemane Jesus demonstrated complete surrender to His Father's will by falling to the ground and praying, *"My Father, if it is possible, may this cup be taken from me. Yet not as I will, but as you will"* (Matthew 26:39).

Jesus asked His loving Father in heaven to deliver Him from going to the cross. But God had a bigger and better plan. By surrendering to God's will, Jesus paid the eternal consequence of your sin and mine. He bore the wrath of God on our behalf, because our Father in heaven never wanted us to suffer the horrible eternal consequences of complete separation from a Holy God. He loves us too much to see us suffer for eternity. Instead, He chose His Son to die in our place. For it is written, *"God so loved the world that He sent His one and only Son so that whoever would believe in Him would not parish but have everlasting life" (John 3:16).*

When you love deeply there can be pain. When you choose to surrender your heart to God, who loves you and created you and was willing to suffer for you, the more you will experience His overwhelming love in the midst of the pain. That love will overflow through you to love others beyond what you can even imagine possible. It requires you to surrender your heart daily to a heavenly Father, believing that He loves and adores you. When you do, you can have the ability to love the unlovable. Look beyond your circumstance. Wait on God with secure confidence that He is allowing whatever situation you're in for a purpose. God can be glorified through the circumstance when you have an eternal perspective.

God showed me that He had a plan through Connor's leukemia. Months prior, He put it on my heart to homeschool my four children. For this reason, I was able to see Connor's symptoms. At the same time, He gave me a month with my other children before my full attention went onto Connor. My children knew they were loved by me and that I was willing to sacrifice my own agenda to dedicate time teaching them. During Connor's illness God showed me for the first time that my children are a gift that I might have to give back to Him sooner than I want. I imagined that if God had asked me before Connor was ever born, *"Do you want a son for five years or not have him at all?"* I would have said, *"Give me my son for five years. I would rather treasure the memories with my precious child for a short period of time than not have him in my life at all."*

During this horrific time of chaos in my home with my marriage struggles and my other children acting out with jealousy and anger, I clung to God's promises. They became my hope. One promise that I recited over and over was, *"He works all things together for the good of those who love Him and are called according to His purpose" (Romans 8:28)*. There was no doubt in my mind that God loved me. The previous year God showed me He was personal through the journey of writing my letters. I knew it was all about a relationship with God, not a religion. The Bible became a personal love letter written just for me. With all my heart I loved Him and I was trying to live my life according to His Word. I wanted to please Him above all else, but I didn't always know how.

Unsure if God would heal Connor this side of heaven, I knew He could. Just months prior, when Mark was unemployed, I studied the book of Genesis where I read about the testimony of Abraham and Isaac. If God had worked in their lives then He would work in mine. Trusting that God loved me and my son, I surrendered Connor on the altar praying for God to heal him, but praying, *"Not my will be done, but Thy will be done,"* remembering how Jesus had prayed in the Garden the night before his crucifixion. This was a test of my heart. Did I really love God above everyone else in my life?

Two days before Christmas we had two of our four children in the hospital. Connor needed a bone marrow transplant. Kayla, our nine-year-old daughter, had prayed that she could save her brother's life. Miraculously, she was an exact tissue match in all six categories, which rarely happens. With no complications Kayla left the hospital the next day.

On Christmas day, after my husband left the hospital to spend the rest of the day with our other three children at home, I sat next to Connor's bed. My heart ached as I watched my precious son with his little bald head asleep on his pillow. Again, I prayed for Jesus to heal him. I asked Him to guide me in the Bible to bring me comfort. As a new Christian, I randomly opened to John 4:43-54 and began reading a passage that I had never read before. Immediately, I related to the story.

The story told of a royal official who left his home town to search for Jesus and when he found Him the official begged for Jesus to come back to his city of Capernaum to heal his sick son. The moment I read these words I looked up toward heaven. God was talking to me. I glanced back to the page and read that Jesus said to the royal official because of his faith, *"You may go, your son will live."* I shook my head in amazement as tears filled my eyes. God had spoken to me through His Word.

Thirteen days later the hospital discharged Connor, the first child to be released so soon after a bone marrow transplant. Connor spent the remainder of his one hundred days of isolation at home with our family. We only visited the hospital for treatment each week as an outpatient. One night as I put Connor to bed, he said, "Mommy, I'm not afraid to die. I can't wait to see Jesus and give God a great big hug." Connor trusted that God loved him and that he would be in a better place. God had another plan for Connor and our family. Within ten months of transplant Connor was off all medications, one year from the date of diagnosis. The doctors at Children's Hospital called him a miracle. Through Connor's battle with leukemia, I experienced God personally as I cried out to my faithful Father in my time of weakness.

Remember, it's not about you. God reveals His power through you to be glorified. The Bible says that God dried up the Red Sea and saved the Israelites from their enemy for a reason, *"He saved them for his name's sake, to make his mighty power known" (Psalm 106:8).* Everything that happens in our lives is for one purpose only, to glorify God and make His power known. It's all about surrendering your life to see God at work through you.

Power of Praise

You can have peace through your pain when you choose to praise and petition God with a thankful heart. Paul and Silas demonstrated this after being stripped, severely beaten, and flogged with a leather whip containing sharp metal pieces that tore apart their flesh. Thrown into prison and carefully guarded, Paul and Silas sang hymns and songs of praise. They prayed to God with thankful hearts.

Can you imagine the agony of gaping wounds? Although in pain, they praised God and everyone heard. Now imagine, while praising God, a violent earthquake caused the prison doors to open up and everyone's chains to fall off. The power of God was revealed through Paul and Silas praising God in their suffering. The Bible says the jailer in charge was ready to take his life, fearing that the prisoners had escaped, and knowing he would face death if they did. But Paul shouted, *"Don't harm yourself! We are all here!"*

The jailer fell trembling at the feet of Paul and Silas asking, *"Sirs, what must I do to be saved?"*

Paul and Silas replied, *"Believe in the Lord Jesus, and you will be saved" (Acts 16:31).* They shared the gospel message to the jailer who accepted Jesus into his heart along with his household. After the jailer washed the wounds of Paul and Silas, he and his family were baptized. The scriptures say that the jailer was filled with the overwhelming joy of the Lord.

Sometimes God asks us to do things that don't make sense from our human perspective. We have to trust Him just as Paul and Silas trusted God and praised Him in the midst of horrendous suffering from unlovable guards who brutally beat and flogged them. Given the opportunity to escape they chose to minister the love of Jesus. The guard and his family were released from their prison of unbelief.

We are all in a prison at some point. Some are in a prison behind bars with cement walls and razor wire, but others face prisons of addiction, sinful thinking, abuse, health issues, difficult relationships, or financial hardships. God will deliver you out of your prison when you seek God's perspective and shift your focus on what's eternal. You may not have endured floggings as Paul and Silas did, but you have survived something. Did God save you from cancer, rape, drugs, an abusive parent, prison, or death? If you're alive, He has preserved your life for a purpose. Trust that God will protect your heart and mind and give you peace that transcends all understanding as you praise Him with a thankful heart. Claim God's promise for peace in the following verses:

Rejoice in the Lord always. I will say it again: Rejoice! Let your gentleness be evident to all. The Lord is near. Do not be anxious about anything, but in everything, by prayer and petition, with thanksgiving, present your requests to God. And the peace of God, which transcends all understanding, will guard your hearts and your minds in Christ Jesus (Phil. 4:4-7).

Do you want peace? If you do, then follow God's recipe. First, rejoice in God. Second, be gentle and kind to everyone knowing that God is with you. Third, thank God for whom He is, what He's done, what He's doing, and even what He's going to do. Fourth, refuse to think on the negative. Recite the promise from above as you trust Him. Fifth, petition God and confess your sin of anxiousness. God will purify you (1 John 1:9). When you do these steps you will have the peace that transcends all understanding in Christ Jesus.

View your situation with the unlovable in light of God's glory and eternity as Paul and Silas did. Proclaim His promise, *"Praise be to the God and Father of our Lord Jesus Christ, who has blessed us in the heavenly realms with every spiritual blessing in Christ" (Eph. 1:3).* Every spiritual blessing includes:

1. You are chosen in Him to be holy and blameless in His sight before the creation of the world (Eph. 1:4).
2. You are adopted into God's family to be His precious child in accordance with His pleasure and will (Eph. 1:5).
3. You are shown the glorious grace of God through His Son, Jesus, who He freely gave to die for you (Eph. 1:6).
4. You are redeemed and forgiven by Jesus' blood (Eph. 1:7).
5. You are lavished with wisdom and understanding (Eph. 1:8).
6. You have been made known the mystery of His will and pleasure in Christ (Eph. 1:9).
7. You are sealed with the Holy Spirit of promise (Eph. 1:13).

You have so much to be thankful for. Rejoice and be glad!

Power to Conquer Fear

What then is holding us back from loving difficult people? For some, it might be fear of persecution. In fact, God talks about fear over 500 times in the King James Version of the Bible. We are not to fear man, but to have a holy and reverent fear of the Lord. We should fear the power and glory of God, the giver and taker of life, but not people. Revere God to find His delight as promised, *"The Lord delights in those who fear [revere] Him, who put their hope in his unfailing love" (Psalm 147:11).*

We will suffer for our faith. God used the apostle Paul to demonstrate and communicate God's power, love, and wisdom in the midst of persecution. God says, *"You do not have a spirit of fear, but of power, love, and sound mind" (2 Timothy 1:7NKJV).* God equips you with supernatural ability to conquer the enemy against all odds. He is your Strength, Refuge, Protector, Warrior, and Friend. He gives you His precious promise in Isaiah to overcome the enemy:

> *'No weapon formed against you shall prosper, and every tongue which rises against you in judgment, you shall condemn. This is the heritage of the servants of the Lord, and their righteousness is from Me,' says the Lord (Isaiah 54:17).*

When you are a servant of the Most High God He will give you discernment, which is the knowledge of good from evil. If you have an uncomfortable feeling, a sense that something is evil and dangerous, listen to that still quiet voice warning you. Have courage to stand up for what God is telling you. Gavin de Becker, a leading expert on violent behavior, warns that many victims sensed danger in the presence of their assailant, but ignored the message of that inner voice. They proceeded to step inside an elevator when they were leery of the man inside, or they allowed someone questionable to assist them with groceries, or they accepted the invitation to go on a date to avoid hurting the guy's feelings. As a result of not listening to their inner voice they suffered violent crimes committed against them.[5]

Never ignore your intuition, gut instinct, or discernment when it comes to a dangerous situation. When God says leave to protect yourself or your kids from violence, then do it. It may save your life like it did Stacy's.

Stacy's Testimony

One evening on the way home from work, for the first time in many years, Stacy turned her eyes to God. In the darkness and pain of her abusive marriage she cried out, *"Where are you? Why have you done this to me? Why have you left me?"*

At that moment Stacy heard a still small voice say, *"I never left you."* There was no doubt in Stacy's mind that God spoke to her. Again she heard His loving voice, *"Leave tonight or you will die."*

Afraid of her abusive husband, she cried out to God, desperate and defeated, *"How can I leave? I can't stand up to him."*

In response, she heard God say, *"Don't be afraid. I am with you."*

Over the past six years Stacy's husband had isolated her from family and friends. He had controlled her from the beginning of their relationship by being possessive of her time. If she wasn't at work, he wanted her with him. At first this attention felt great. Stacy had felt abandoned by her parents through divorce and was sexually abused by family members. Growing up she felt worthless and dirty. She married a man who treated her poorly, thinking that's what she deserved. Eventually the possessiveness and control turned into emotional and physical abuse that paralyzed Stacy. Fortunately, Stacy had a career that provided her a sense of worth and financial security. But this had never given her the confidence to leave before. It wasn't until hearing the still quiet voice of God that she had courage.

At home, Stacy had boldness for the first time. She started packing her things. She said the words, "I'm leaving and it's over." But her husband wasn't going to allow her to leave without a fight. He raped and beat her. In an outrage he refused to let her take anything with her. Holding her by the hair at gunpoint he made her sign a piece of paper that gave up her rights to have any of their possessions. Although she had worked hard in her career to contribute financially to their beautiful home, she left it all behind with only the clothes on her back.

Stacy drove away to start a new life after six years of abuse. What took her so long to leave? She was afraid for her life until she realized that God was with her. Today, Stacy looks back and sees how God protected her and gave her boldness to leave. Even though she was raped by her husband, she rejoices that he never killed her. She's alive today. She knows God saved her. Not only did He save her from further torment from an unstable and abusive man, God provided for her every need as she depended on Him completely.

Subconsciously, Stacy never felt worthy of a respectful man and she never would have married the well-adjusted man that she later did if it wasn't for a friend who spoke truth to her in love. Her friend boldly told her that she deserved a quality man and to stop dating disrespectful men like her ex-husband. Finally, someone cared enough to give Stacy godly counsel, to tell her she was valuable, and to point out the patterns that she was falling back into.

Stacy listened and God restored her with a loving man. Yet for years Stacy lived in fear that her ex-husband would find her and kill her. Once Stacy invited Jesus into her heart God completely healed her and gave her confidence that she was protected by the power of the Holy Spirit. Stacy forgave her ex-husband and she has prayed often for his healing and salvation. Who knows? Her abusive ex-husband may be a Christian today. What we do know is that by God's grace Stacy was plucked out of that abusive marriage to give her a new life and to start a new legacy with her own family, fully devoted to loving God.

Power of God's Promises

People may argue with you, accuse you, and abuse you. Knowing who you are in Christ will prevent these attacks from penetrating your heart, although they still may hurt. Nevertheless, we should not be defined by our feelings or what others say or do to us. Instead we should know and claim God's promises. Be self-controlled and alert.

The enemy is prowling around whispering lies in your ear to pull your conversation off-track. Hold your thoughts captive. Don't allow your mind to be tempted to think on what's evil. Instead, think on God's promises to overcome the enemy, for He says,

> *He has given us His very great and precious promises, so that through them you may participate in the divine nature and escape the corruption in the world caused by evil desires (2 Peter 1:4).*

Recognize the spiritual battle vying to keep you from God. The only way to conquer the enemy is with God's truth. In fact, in the following scripture from Ephesians, your faith will extinguish the flaming arrows of the evil one. Those arrows come in the form of lies about ourselves and others. Verbal attacks, false accusations, put-downs, gossip, and fear work to defeat our effectiveness to bring honor and glory to God. Our best weapon is to arm ourselves every day to fight against the enemy who tries to rob us from God's peace, joy, and purpose. Read what God says about the battle we're in.

> *Finally, be strong in the Lord and in his mighty power. Put on the full armor of God, so that you can take your stand against the devil's schemes. For our struggle is not against flesh and blood, but against the rulers, against the authorities, against the powers of this dark world and against the spiritual forces of evil in the heavenly realms (Ephesians 6:10-13).*

Do you notice that our battles are not against the unlovable people in our lives? Do you see that God's Word warns you that your struggle is not against flesh and blood? Sisters and Brothers, this is important to remember. This is the truth of God. You are in a spiritual battle. The enemy is feeding you lies, he whispers in your ear, he brings up your past, he puts fear and doubt in your mind, he knows your weaknesses, he tempts you to sin and fall away from God, he wants to destroy your testimony and make you live in the bondage of guilt and shame and fear and pride.

93

The devil will make sin enticing without telling you the consequences of that sin. He observes the choices you make and the words you say to tempt you in your areas of weakness. The devil will tell you that you have a need that God can't meet. Just like when Adam and Eve were tempted in the Garden, the serpent convinced them that God was holding out on them. This is precisely why you must put on the full armor of God to defeat the devil and those he uses to take you away from God. Read Ephesians 6:14-18 about the pieces of armor that you must put on to go into battle as a soldier of Christ. Take the following steps every day to fight your battle:

1. **Stand firm with the belt of truth buckled around your waist.** Satan wants you to believe his lies, but stand firm with Jesus who will fight your battle. Jesus answered, *"I am the way and the truth and the life. No one comes to the Father except through me" (John 14:6).* Jesus spoke creation into existence. John 1:14 says, *"The Word of God became flesh and made His dwelling among us. We have seen His glory, the glory of the One and Only, who came from the Father, full of grace and truth."*

2. **Put on the breastplate of righteousness.** Satan wants you to think that sin has no consequences, but know that sin leads to destruction and spiritual death. Your obedience to God will protect you against the consequences of unrighteous behavior. Don't let the enemy devise schemes through unlovable people to distract you from God and His plans and purposes for your life. Stay obedient for God to show Himself to you (John 14:21).

3. **Have your feet fitted with readiness with the gospel of peace.** Satan wants us to live in fear and be anxious, but when we know what Christ did on the cross we stand firm in our salvation, ready to share the reason for our peace. We can feel safe and secure knowing that God is with us and in us and for us. His peace is evident through our gentleness with unlovable people.

4. **Carry the shield of faith that extinguishes the flaming arrows of the evil one.** Faith in God is complete trust that He loves you and desires the very best for you. Satan wants you to doubt God and His promises, but I beg you to believe and trust God in whatever circumstance you face. Christ loves you and He's got your back.

5. **Wear the helmet of salvation.** The helmet represents your mind, what you believe and your thoughts. Satan wants you to forget who you are in Christ Jesus. Claim the truth that you have the power of *"Christ in you, the hope of glory."* You have the mind of Christ (Colossians 1:27, 1 Cor. 2:16). You can do all things through Christ who strengthens you (Phil. 4:13).

6. **Wield the sword of the Spirit.** The Word is powerful and life giving. We command authority and power when we speak the Word of God in our prayers. Meditate on His Word to stand secure and confident in Christ against the devil's schemes. If Jesus created life by the spoken Word then God's Word gives life when we speak it out loud.

Proclaim God's promises in your prayers to penetrate the lies of the enemy with the truth of God. Look at the benefits of living by the power of God's Word:

> ➤ The Word of God keeps us from sinning (Psalm 119:11).
> ➤ The Word of God is living and active (Hebrews 4:12).
> ➤ The Word of God nourishes us like bread (Deut. 8:3).
> ➤ The Word of God guides our path (Psalm 119:105).
> ➤ The Word of God is flawless (Proverbs 30:5).
> ➤ The Word of God is Jesus (John 1:14).
> ➤ The Word of God is truth (John 17:17).
> ➤ The Word of God is life (Phil. 2:16).

From these scriptures you can see the power of God's Word. Therefore, you should hide it in your heart to gain the power you need to overcome your adversity and to keep you from sinning against God.

Just as Jesus used the Word of God when Satan tempted Him, the Word of God will disarm the lies of the enemy and those who come against you. *PRAY to unleash God's power.* Jesus promises,

> *If you remain in me and my words remain in you, ask whatever you wish, and it will be given you. This is to my Father's glory, that you bear much fruit, showing yourselves to be my disciples (John 15:7-8).*

Unleash the power of God when you ask with the right motives. When you remain in Jesus and His Word in you, you will ask according to His purpose to bear much fruit, showing yourself as His disciple. Your prayers will glorify Him. Believe that God will eventually answer your prayer to bring your unlovable into a relationship with Christ. It's imperative for you to stand firm against temptation in order to remain in God's will for the purpose to advance His Kingdom. Our confidence to overcome the enemy comes from preparation. That preparation requires us to read and feast upon the Word to be nourished by it. Through meditating on his word we are able to proclaim the powerful truth out loud through prayer. We are able to resist the devil and his schemes that cause division in our relationship with God and His people.

Power of the Holy Spirit

We belong to Christ to be empowered by Him to love unlovable people. His promise in Romans 5:5 says, *"And hope does not disappoint us, because God has poured out his love into our hearts by the Holy Spirit, whom he has given us."* Claim the promise that you have the power to love. He would never tell us to love if we were incapable of loving. God wants us to be His instrument, His vessel, and the hands and feet of Jesus to love the difficult people in our lives.

The Holy Spirit gives you the same supernatural power that raised Jesus from the grave. This truth should give you confidence in God. Remember you belong to the Most High God, Creator of the heavens and earth, who loves you. When you are equipped with God's power, no harm will come that God doesn't allow for His purpose and glory. Think about this, God will do a miracle in your life in order for you to proclaim His faithfulness. A good example of this is when we saw the power of God come upon the disciples to testify to the gospel.

At first, Peter denied Christ three times for fear of persecution when Jesus was arrested. After Peter witnessed the death, resurrection, and ascension of Christ, he was empowered with the Holy Spirit on the day of Pentecost. Without fear of even death He shared the hope of Jesus for the rest of his life until he was tortured and hung upside down on a cross for preaching the good news. God's Word says in Acts 1:8, *"You will receive power when the Holy Spirit comes on you; and you will be my witnesses in Jerusalem, and in all Judea and Samaria, and to the ends of the earth."* Pray that God would increase the power of the Holy Spirit inside of you to love the difficult people in your life.

Power of Jesus' name

When Jesus walked on earth two thousand years ago, He sent seventy of His followers ahead of Him two by two to prepare the way for His coming. He warned them that He was sending them out like lambs among wolves and told them to enter homes and proclaim peace. He said that if a man of peace lived there it would rest on him, but if they were not welcome then the peace would return to them. Jesus commissioned the men to heal the sick and tell people that the kingdom of God is near. The seventy returned to Jesus with joy, saying,

> *'Lord, even the demons submit to us in your name.' He replied, 'I saw Satan fall like lightning from heaven. I have given you authority to trample on snakes and scorpions and to overcome all the power of the enemy; nothing will harm you. However, do not rejoice that the spirits submit to you, but rejoice that your names are written in heaven' (Luke 10:17-20).*

In other words, you defeat Satan with the name of Jesus. With that ability it is far better that you rejoice that you are saved and spending eternity in heaven than boast in what you can do here on earth with the power that Jesus gives you. Jesus demonstrated His power here on earth by healing the sick, giving sight to the blind, and casting out demons. According to Jesus, we have God's power. Yet with that power we ought to take greater satisfaction that we belong to Christ.

Unleash the power of God using the name of Jesus for miracles to happen. Peter healed the crippled beggar that sat by the city gate day after day. When the beggar asked Peter and John for money Peter replied that he had no silver or gold but he had something far greater. He had the Holy Spirit living in him. Peter had the power of God. That power was released when Peter trusted in the name of Jesus to heal the beggar. He gives all credit, honor, and glory to God in the following verse:

By faith in the name of Jesus, this man whom you see and know was made strong. It is Jesus' name and the faith that comes through Him that has given this complete healing to him, as you can all see (Acts 3:16).

There were three things that Peter did that healed the crippled beggar. Peter prayed specifically, he prayed in the name of Jesus, and he trusted that Jesus would heal the man. Peter never took the credit, but gave glory to God. The same God will answer your prayers and when He does you should testify to His faithfulness. Consider that our sovereign all-knowing God knows whether we will tell others about His faithfulness before He answers our prayers. Maybe that's why He answers some prayers with a yes and others with a no. Is God waiting for you to trust Him and proclaim His faithfulness to others? He may be waiting to give you the desires of your heart. Are you willing to give Him glory for all answered prayers regardless of whether He answers them according to your ways?

God says, *"The name of the Lord is a strong tower. The righteous run to it and are safe" (Proverbs 18:10).* Are you righteous? You are if you've made Jesus your Lord. Covered by the blood of Jesus, God sees you perfect and righteous like Jesus. There is power when your identity is in Jesus. Boldly call on His name when you face trials of any kind. People may think you're crazy, but that's alright. Better to be protected by God than attempt to protect your image. Be a Jesus freak! Do not be ashamed of Jesus. If you are unwilling to stand up for Jesus and proclaim your faith by calling on His name then why should He stand up to defend you before the throne of God on Judgment Day?

You are saved! The Bible says, *"Everyone who calls on the name of the Lord will be saved" (Acts 2:21).* Of course this scripture is talking about saved from eternal separation from God. We have no guarantee that God will save us from physical harm or death here on earth when we call on His name. In fact, many followers of Christ have been put to death over the past two thousand years. Honestly, I don't know if they called on the name of Jesus to be saved. Stephen in the New Testament of Acts chapter seven cried out for Jesus to take him as he prayed for God to forgive those who stoned him before he died. God used this incident as a witness to further the gospel as He does with many martyrs.

People see God's power through the strength of those who endure great suffering with the joyful hope of heaven and continued love for their abuser. You may never have to suffer the way many of our sisters and brothers have been tortured in the past and are suffering around the world today. In many Muslim, Communist, and Socialistic countries people cannot share their love for Jesus openly and proclaim what the Word of God teaches without facing the possibility of personal or financial harm, imprisonment, or even death. The devil is using fear tactics to muzzle God's people.

Be bold and courageous to call on the name of Jesus. When facing trouble in the Old Testament, King Asa of Judah called on the name of the Lord and God gave him success against the Cushites, recorded in 2 Chronicles 14:11-12. Again, in the Old Testament, God granted favor to Elisha who called on the name of the Lord when he was being harassed by jeering youth (2 Kings 2:24). Forty-two unruly and mocking teenagers were mauled by two bears to learn the lesson not to mess with God's people!

We know how bears can be fierce animals, but God gave me peace when I faced a mother bear with her cub in the forest. At a Christian retreat I walked with a new friend through the mountains in Canada.

We noticed the mama bear about thirty yards away standing on her hind legs, while her cub scurried up a tree. I rejoiced and called on the name of Jesus for protection with my hands automatically raised, since I often had prayed that way. In that moment I had no fear, but instead, I delighted and marveled at the sight of God's creation until my new friend nudged me to leave. She probably thought I was a little crazy and that's alright. Today I testify to God's faithfulness.

With that being said, God built my faith as a new believer hearing the testimonies of what God had done in people's lives. One of the first testimonies I heard concerning the power of Jesus' name was from a woman who had been attacked in her home by an intruder. The man grabbed her neck when this petite woman proclaimed with authority, "In Jesus' name let me go." The big man fell back. Again he attacked her. Again he fell back when she said the name of Jesus. The intruder left her home when she commanded him to do so by the power of Jesus' name. He went running and I like to imagine that he's a believer today.

The previous story is not an isolated event. Many people have told me stories of being saved from violent circumstances. One woman was saved from a rapist who crawled through an open window one night. The intruder was on top of her when she screamed over and over, "Help me Jesus!" and the man went running. In the following scripture God says speak His name and He will send angels to protect you.

For he will command his angels concerning you to guard you in all your ways; they will lift you up in their hands, so that you will not strike your foot against a stone...'Because he loves me,' says the Lord, 'I will rescue him; I will protect him, for he acknowledges my name' (Psalm 91:11-14).

Can I guarantee that you won't be hurt in a dangerous situation? No, but I can tell you that if you love Jesus and believe in the power of Jesus' name and His strength, and you are bold enough to call on Him, I believe He will come to your rescue. Try it! What do you have to lose? If you die tragically you will be with your Savior in heaven if you have surrendered your life to Him. That is the hope we have in Jesus.

In the Old Testament, God spoke to Joshua before he led the people across the Jordan River into the Promised Land to gain their inheritance He swore to his ancestors. God said, *"Be strong and courageous. Do not be afraid; do not be discouraged, for the Lord your God will be with you wherever you go" (Joshua 1:7-9).* We have that same promise. God remains the same yesterday, today, and tomorrow. God is with you. His love for you is far beyond what you can comprehend. Ponder the fact that He Himself would take residence within you to equip you with His strength, His wisdom, and His comfort all for His glory. Jesus told his disciples that He was going away to return to His Father and that the Holy Spirit, the Counselor, would come to be with them. Jesus said these words, *"I have told you these things, so that in Me you may have peace. In this world you will have trouble. But take heart! I have overcome the world" (John 16:33).* Jesus is alive. Resurrection power is available to you. Do not be afraid to proclaim His power!

Dear Mighty God, I praise you that I can do all things through Christ who strengthens me. Your grace is sufficient for me as your power is made perfect in my weakness. I boast in my weaknesses so that Christ's power may rest on me. I surrender my circumstance to you that your will be done, not my will. For I know that you work all things together for the good to those who love you and are called according to your purpose. I rejoice in you Lord for you are near. I will be anxious about nothing, but I thank you for _____ as I present my requests to you that I may have the peace of God, which transcends all understanding that guards my heart and mind in Christ Jesus. I do not have a spirit of fear, but of power, love, and sound mind. No weapon formed against me shall prosper. I am strong in your mighty power as I put on the full armor of God, so that I can take my stand against the devil's schemes. For my struggles are not against flesh and blood, but against the powers of this dark world and against the evil forces in the heavenly realms. By faith in the name of Jesus I give you my relationship with _____ and pray for complete healing so that you may be glorified. Thank you for saving me to make your mighty power known. I fear no evil for you are my strong tower and I will be saved.

101

You command your angels concerning me to guard me in all my ways. Because I love you, you will rescue me and protect me as I pray in Jesus' name. Amen.
Phil. 4:13; 2 Cor. 12:8-11; Matthew 26:39; Romans 8:28; Psalm 106:8; Phil. 4:4-7; 2Timothy 1:7NKJV; Ephesians 6:10-13; Isaiah 54:17; Proverbs 18:10; Psalm 91:11-14.

GOD'S TRANSFORMING TRUTH
Proclaim your power to conquer fear: "For God has not given us a spirit of fear, but of power and of love and of a sound mind." (2Timothy 1:7NKJV)

QUESTION TO PONDER
According to God's Word, who do you wage war against in this world?

TAKE ACTION
Rise in the morning to put on the full armor of God with praise, prayer, and proclamation of His promises in the name of Jesus.

Chapter Six

Overcome Evil with Blessing

*Do not repay evil with evil or insult with insult, but
with blessing, because to this you were called so
that you may inherit a blessing.*
1 Peter 3:9

Not until my thirties did I come to know the woman who replaced my
grandmother. Great Aunt Daisy never wanted children of her own.
Nevertheless at the age of forty she insisted on raising her two young
nieces when their mother died of ovarian cancer. One of those girls was
my mother.

Great Aunt Daisy turned ninety-two years old when I got close
enough to discover the facade of the critical aunt who kept me distant.
Her strong opinions and harsh comments intimidated me as a young
girl and into adulthood. Diagnosed with a cancerous tumor in her
uterus, she became dependent on others for the first time in her life.
The looming possibility of Great Aunt Daisy's death created
meaningful conversations between my mother and me regarding her
experiences growing up with her aunt. While I discovered these stories,
my appreciation and curiosity grew for the woman who sacrificed to
raise my mother and her younger sister.

In response to Great Aunt Daisy's illness, God directed me to write
my very first letter to her. With honesty, I spoke truth in love. I shared
my feelings of sadness that I missed out on having a close relationship
with her while I was growing up, that I kept my distance due to her

overbearing ways. Yet at the time I started writing the letter I had no idea how much she influenced my life.

As I prayed, God revealed the impact she had on me. With gratitude I expressed my appreciation for her willingness to teach me how to sew that directed my career path in the fashion industry years later. I wrote about stories I remembered from childhood and cherished memories my mother shared with me about growing up with her aunt. These stories brought tears to Daisy's eyes as I read the letter to her one morning, which cast some light into her dreary days alone. She had isolated herself from family and friends by her abrasive and rude behavior.

The process of writing the letter turned into a desire for my mother and me to record Daisy's stories. Taping her stories inspired conversations that uncovered the past pain of her childhood and brought understanding of the aunt who should have been a loving grandmother figure to me when I was growing up.

The respect we showed Great Aunt Daisy, by expressing an interest in her life, softened her heart towards us. As her abrasive attitude changed, we delighted in her insightful thoughts, intriguing stories, and humorous comments. The broken relationship between my mother and her aunt, created by years of Aunt Daisy's rejection and criticism, evolved to a place of deep appreciation and devotion. The Bible says, *"Rise in the presence of the aged, show respect for the elderly and revere your God" (Leviticus 19:32).* Our efforts to spend time with Great Aunt Daisy demonstrated respect for her and in doing so we glorified God and our lives were changed.

When Daisy was asked whether we could record her stories, she responded emphatically, "Well, how else will you be remembered by posterity if you don't open up your trap and talk?"

Our brazen Aunt Daisy was right! To be known and remembered we must share our stories. But to be honest, there were many times I would rather visit a friend during my brief visits to my hometown. If I went by my feelings I would have given up on Great Aunt Daisy a long time before. Especially the times she criticized my hair, the clothes I wore, or the time she hung up the phone after shouting that I interrupted her evening news. Instead of retaliating by avoiding her or responding defensively, God gave me the ability to forgive her and to persevere with patience and kindness. After time, my mother and I were blessed when we sacrificed our selfish agendas to hear her stories, to understand our heritage of the people we came from, the beliefs we have, and the reasons we made some of the decisions we did in the past.

For this reason, I strongly encourage listening to the stories of difficult and unlovable people, no matter how they may respond at first. The next chapter *Wise-Up to Understand* will explain in further detail the blessing of knowing the difficult person's past pain as well as their perspective and personality. There's also an added benefit to taking the time to listen to the stories of your difficult parent. Not only can you learn from their past, you can honor them to receive the blessing that God promises in the Ten Commandments to honor your father and your mother so that you will enjoy long life and that life may go well for you (Exodus 20:12).

Overcome evil with blessing to receive every spiritual blessing. When you repay evil or unkind behavior with blessings you will be amazed at how God will bless you. God's Word promises,

> *Do not repay evil with evil or insult with insult, but with blessing, because to this you were called so that you may inherit a blessing (1 Peter 3:9).*

Understand that Jesus repaid evil with blessing as He sacrificed His life to die for you and me when we were still sinners. He forgives us and He asks us to forgive those who sin against us as discussed in the chapter *Forgive to be Set Free*. His obedience gave Him resurrection power to persevere to the point of death on a cross. You have that same resurrection power to overcome evil with blessing through the Holy Spirit. Your obedience will be rewarded with the glory of everlasting life and the *fruits of the Spirit of love, joy, peace, patience, kindness, goodness, faithfulness, gentleness, and self-control (Gal. 5:16-23)*. He fills you with an overwhelming sense of the Holy Spirit as you love the unlovable when they don't deserve it.

When you realize the amazing blessing of what Jesus did for you on the cross, you can respond to others out of a deep appreciation for what He has done. Consider that when you bless the unlovable you bless God. *Jesus said that what you do to the least of these you have done to Him and you will be blessed (Matthew 25:40).* Jesus demonstrated how to overcome evil with blessing when unrighteous men came to arrest Him.

When Jesus' followers saw what was going to happen, they said, "Lord, should we strike with our swords?" And one of them struck the servant of the high priest, cutting off his right ear. But Jesus answered, "No more of this!" And he touched the man's ear and healed him (Luke 22:49-51).

Instead of lashing out with anger, Jesus took the time to heal the man's ear. This was one of the men who intended to put chains on Jesus and lead Him to his death. This act of kindness illustrates how Jesus repaid evil with blessing to win them over to God. Who knows how that servant of the high priest would be changed by the act of compassion Jesus demonstrated. Notice that although Jesus repaid evil with kindness, He still had to suffer a brutal death. His blessing came when he was resurrected from the dead and ascended to heaven and was seated at the right hand of the Father (Acts 2:33). Of course, as a Christian our ultimate blessing is the reward of heaven, but not only is this true, we are set free to experience the abundant life on earth that Christ offers through our obedience to repay evil with blessing.

Bless through Prayer

One of the greatest ways we can bless someone who is difficult is through prayer. Before spending time together pray for them. In fact, my mother and I often asked God to go before us when we spent time with Great Aunt Daisy. We asked God to soften her heart and to reveal Himself to her through us. We asked Him to guide and direct our conversation with wisdom on how to love her. We saw God's faithfulness over time. One of the fondest memories my mother and her sister have with their aunt was toward the end of Aunt Daisy's life. In Daisy's convalescent room my mother suggested they pray together. During the prayer their once abrasive and critical aunt piped-up to tell God how thankful she was for her two nieces whom she loved.

When we pray for others we are blessed in return. We get to become part of a miracle. Consider asking a difficult person, *"How can I pray for you?"* Often their demeanor will soften. Usually the person who is unlovable is hurting inside; dealing with physical, emotional, or spiritual pain. We express that we care when we ask if we can pray. With more understanding of what's going on we can offer compassion instead of judgment.

A few years ago, a woman walked by me at the elementary school my children attended when I heard her snap bitterly at her children. At first, I judged her. Then I noticed her clutching her back as she walked slowly. When I asked if she was in pain, she told me that she pulled a muscle. I expressed compassion and told her I would pray for her. Her attitude changed as I empathized with her pain.

The next time I saw her I remembered her name, told her I had prayed for her to be healed, and asked how she was feeling. This woman was overjoyed with gratitude that a stranger would take the time to pray. We can change a life when we offer to pray. When you ask, consider praying on the spot for them. If they feel awkward or uncomfortable then lift them up silently. Most of the time, you will be surprised how your thoughtfulness can change their heart and brighten your day. Do something good by offering to pray.

Bless by Speaking Truth

Expect conflict with those who do not have a personal relationship with Jesus. When it comes to matters concerning the Word of God, unbelievers may not be able to hear or understand what the believer is saying because they do not have the Holy Spirit to give them insight, wisdom, and discernment. Jesus answered the question why some people could not understand what He was teaching:

Why is my language not clear to you? Because you are unable to hear what I say. You belong to your father, the devil, and you want to carry out your father's desire. He was a murderer from the beginning, not holding to the truth, for there is no truth in him. When he lies, he speaks his native language, for he is a liar and the father of lies. Yet because I tell the truth, you do not believe me (John 8:43-45).

People are deceived by the enemy of this world. We either belong to God or we belong to the devil. We make a choice every day to be a friend with God or an enemy of God by how we demonstrate our love for people. Our decision to love people applies not only to those who believe but those who are deaf to the message of God. Those who do not have the Holy Spirit living in them may not understand God's truth, because Satan has blinded them and caused them not to hear, so that they cannot see the glory of Christ (2 Cor. 4:4).

Before my husband became a Christian he called me a Jesus freak. At first I was insulted then I realized there was no greater compliment to receive. After Mark became a Christian he gave his testimony at church and said, "I hope someday people will call me a Jesus freak like I called my wife." Mark confessed that it was my gentle spirit, despite his harshness, that won him over to Christ. At the same time, I could not help but share the hope of Jesus that I had received.

You've probably heard the saying, "kill him with kindness" when dealing with difficult people. This concept hints to the faithful promise to overcome evil with blessing to inherit a blessing. Your kindness will melt their heart. You will reap the reward of sowing for good not evil. God says, *"The one who sows to please his sinful nature, from that nature will reap destruction; the one who sows to please the Spirit, from the Spirit will reap eternal life" (Galatians 6:8).* God will reward you for blessing the unlovable.

Bless with Your Testimony

Remember the woman at the well who shared her testimony of how she met Jesus and many people were saved. We can lead people to Jesus by sharing our testimony, which means we glorify God by telling others about what He is doing in our lives. Imagine what our lives might be like if we let every circumstance be an opportunity to rejoice in what God is doing or going to do. Trust that God is in control of the situation and that He is allowing the struggle for the purpose to tell others about His faithfulness. God's word reminds us the proper way we should behave as Christians:

> *Let love be without hypocrisy. Abhor what is evil. Cling to what is good. Be kindly affectionate to one another with brotherly love, in honor giving preference to one another; not lagging in diligence, fervent in spirit, serving the Lord; rejoicing in hope, patient in tribulation, continuing steadfastly in prayer; distributing to the needs of the saints, given to hospitality. Bless those who persecute you; bless and do not curse (Romans 12:9-14 NKJV).*

When we follow Jesus and talk about Him the enemy will come against us. The darkness doesn't like the light. You are the light of Jesus. You will sense through the Holy Spirit when someone dislikes you. Often when you sense their disapproval, they are living in sin. The sin may be pride that they don't need God, unbelief that there is only one way to God, or fear that you will try to convert them to Christianity or condemn their lifestyle. Sometimes you don't need to address someone's sin to convict him or her. When you share your testimony of what God is doing in your life the Holy Spirit can convict that person. Let me illustrate with a story.

Gail's Testimony

A few years ago, Gail called herself a Christian and at one time went to church. During her divorce she dated another man and became sexually involved, attending church less frequently. Her sin separated her from God and her Christian friends. Every time I saw Gail I could tell she avoided me. I continued to embrace her without condemnation. I would simply share what God was doing in my life. At that time, Mark was unemployed. I shared with Gail how God provided and the miracles He was doing.

I continued to lift Gail up in prayer for God to reveal truth to her about her sin. Finally, God took the veil off. Gail was convicted of her sexual immorality. Later she told me, "Kirsten, every time I saw you I could only take this much of you," she held up her thumb and pointer finger measuring a quarter of an inch. We laughed. Gail admitted that when she was living an ungodly lifestyle she never wanted me around. When she saw me she felt convicted of her sin. She couldn't understand my joy until she realized that Jesus died for her sin of fornication and adultery. Gail thought she was a Christian, but she never truly understood the significance of her salvation, that *she* nailed Jesus to the cross. God patiently waited for her to repent and make Jesus the Lord of her life. When she did, we praised God and rejoiced for what He was doing in both our lives.

If you proclaim Christ and stand for righteousness, you will likely be shunned, insulted, or even attacked for your faith. Rejoice in your suffering knowing that the enemy feels threatened by the power of God's testimony through you, and the difference you're making for the kingdom of God. God says, *"They [God's people in the last days] overcame him [Satan] by the blood of the Lamb [Jesus] and by the word of their testimony" (Revelation 12:11).* God's people can conquer Satan and his stronghold on people when they glorify God and share what He has done and is doing in their lives by the power of Jesus death and resurrection. Our courage to share and our confidence in Christ will minister to the hearts of hurting people and they will often turn to Christ to be saved.

God encourages us not to shrink back in fear of death or persecution or insult from those who accuse us. The enemy will attempt to thwart our efforts, but stand firm to be blessed. Read the following promise from God:

Blessed are you when people insult you, persecute you and falsely say all kinds of evil against you because of me. Rejoice and be glad, because great is your reward in heaven, for in the same way they persecuted the prophets who were before you (Matthew 5:11-12).

You may ask *how is it possible to rejoice and be glad in the midst of dealing with cruel people.* Only through a relationship with Christ can we rejoice in our suffering with the understanding that this life is our temporary dwelling place. We have the hope of heaven and the power of the Holy Spirit. Our heavenly Father comforts, strengthens, and empowers us to a new level of intimacy with Him when we overcome evil with blessing.

Trust that God will avenge those who hurt you and your loved ones. God says, *"Do not take revenge, my friends, but leave room for God's wrath, for it is written: 'It is mine to avenge; I will repay,' says the Lord" (Romans 12:19).* God is our Judge. He is a just and fair God. This is not to say that justice should not be served. Of course we have a judicial system to make sure people abide by the laws and suffer the consequences of their crimes. Consequences allow people to learn and grow. We can trust that God will use the authorities in place to serve justice. Ultimately, we let people off our hook to place them on God's hook knowing He will discipline those who need it. And at the same time, we can be grateful that as Christians we do not suffer God's wrath on Judgment Day, yet we may be disciplined for our offenses here on earth. Sometimes the biggest blessing we can give is to discipline those who are disobedient, which will be taught in the chapter *STOP to Handle Anger*.

Often we love people in the way that feels most comfortable for us. When this happens, it's like spinning our tires on the ice and not getting anywhere. In fact, you could end up drained of energy trying to do something that means nothing to that person. Gary Chapman in his well respected book *The Five Love Languages* helps people identify their primary style of receiving and showing love, which helped to inspire the rest of this chapter. Loving difficult people in a way that's meaningful to them can be a challenge in many relationships. We think

111

of ourselves. We do what's easy instead of focusing on the other person. To go outside our comfort zone is hard work. But when we do, we demonstrate true love. Imagine what could happen if we sacrificed our own agenda to be uncomfortable to do what will mean the most to the unlovable. That's true love.[6]

Bless with Time

Those who feel most loved by spending time together can feel most rejected by a lack of time together. This is intensified when there's a disagreement and their response may be to pull away, retract in self-preservation, or lash out due to hurt feelings, which worsens the situation because they push everyone away. What the person who enjoys your time is really saying, "Come be with me I need us to spend time together." My great Aunt Daisy was a good example of someone who pushed people away with her abrasiveness, often intensified through alcohol, yet the way she felt most loved was spending time with her. She was hurt and resentful when no one wanted to be with her.

If your unlovable person is complaining that you're never at home or that they never see you, then stop to evaluate if spending time together might be the way they feel most loved. Consider investing time with that person and you may experience a positive difference in their behavior and attitude toward you, like we did with our Great Aunt Daisy.

Bless with Touch

Touch is powerful. It melts cold and icy hearts away. We need physical touch to survive. In societies where children are orphaned and not touched they have been known to die. Physical touch is not about sex. It's about showing affection. For some, it's not as natural to touch due to sexual abuse or rarely experiencing touch growing up. Nevertheless true love sacrifices what feels comfortable to do what is meaningful for the other person. Be sensitive and aware of body language that will communicate if touch is well received. At first it may feel awkward, but as time goes on hugs become natural.

In the car with my teenage son, he loves when I touch his head, back, or arm. When he's grumpy after a long day at school, he lights up by my touch. In fact, God did a work in my heart to sacrifice my own selfish desires to meet my son's need. Remember, I once had an aversion to feet? God tested me in this area. Watching TV, Cameron asked if I would rub his feet. Initially my response was, "No way! I hate feet, especially dirty feet." With that being said, the next time he asked, his feet were clean. What are you willing to do to demonstrate your love? I was amazed at what happened when it was no longer about me but reaching out to others with physical touch to express my love. Often a lack of affection will drive someone to go where they can get it. Today, I believe we can eliminate the high rate of premarital sex and teen pregnancy by slowing down to hug and cuddle with our teenagers.

Bless with Treasures

Some people value each gift as a special treasure or token of love no matter how expensive. But the person whose love language is not gifts will likely be unimpressed. My clue that gifts were unimportant to me was when I realized most of the gifts my husband gave me I returned for what I really wanted. Eventually my husband and I agreed not to give one another gifts. Neither of us experienced joy and satisfaction by receiving them. We took the stress out of the holidays by eliminating wasteful time and money spent on unwanted presents.

If you have someone in your life who feels loved through gifts, then take note of the kinds of things they choose for themselves, or the things they like to collect, or even talk about wanting. Pay attention to the details in their life to help you minister to them through gifts. If all else fails, don't be afraid to ask them specifically what kind of gifts they most enjoy receiving. Melt bitterness away by giving the message *I'm thinking about you and I love you.*

Bless with Service

God reminds us in Galatians 5:13 we are to love people by serving them. The apostle Paul said, *"You, my brothers, were called to be free. But do not use your freedom to indulge the sinful nature; rather, serve one another in love."* To be a Christian is to serve through acts of kindness as Jesus demonstrated by washing His disciple's feet. As you serve it's important to be aware of your motives. Are you serving to be recognized and elevated or are you serving with a humble heart thinking of others as better than yourself?

In some cultures the mother-in-law can serve her family with a superior attitude projecting to the daughter-in-law that she is not good enough for her son. These wives feel ridiculed, inferior, and inadequate by the overbearing mother-in-law who insists everything be done her way. Under the guise of serving, the mother creates animosity in the relationship whether intentional or not. If this is happening in your family, instead of competing to win approval or stew in frustration, the better solution is to express appreciation for her willingness to help. If you need to have a conversation about put-downs or sarcasm or underhanded remarks then use the guide from the chapter *Express Truth in Love*. Also, try to discover how she feels most loved and start loving her that way.

Realize that people may serve you because they do what is comfortable for them. This is a good way to determine the way someone feels most loved. Look at what they do for you. Their efforts might mean nothing to you if your love language is different than theirs. Yet by accepting the service of others, it will allow them to feel good about themselves. Even if you don't need their help, you can appreciate their efforts.

Bless with Affirmation

As mentioned in the chapter *Motivated by a Pure Heart*, everyone wants to hear positive words. They want to feel adored and cherished. The way we can do this is by speaking sweet words of affection. For example, claiming them as your beloved through statements to the person like, "How's *my* little boy?" even when he's 16. Or "How's *my* mother-in-law today?" "What's *my* friend doing today?" "When do I get to see *my* hubby?" Your words are saying you belong to me and I love you. For some people their heart overflows when they are recognized as your special person, acknowledged for their efforts and good deeds, for their thoughts and opinions, and for the way they look. The opposite happens when we use discouraging words, put downs, or body language that communicates disapproval. Many people can feel defeated and unloved by someone who argues or disagrees or fails to listen and affirm. That's why we need to be attentive through eye contact and nodding to acknowledge what is being said. Not that you have to agree, but being heard is of great value to all of us. Choosing your words carefully will be well received, especially by people who feel most loved through affirmation. Remember God will reward your good deeds, just as He will avenge those who do evil. All we have to be concerned about is what we do to honor our Lord as it is written:

Repay no one evil for evil. Have regard for good things in the sight of all men. If it is possible, as much as depends on you, live peaceably with all men. Beloved, do not avenge yourselves, but rather give place to wrath; for it is written, "Vengeance is Mine, I will repay," says the Lord. Therefore "If your enemy is hungry, feed him; If he is thirsty, give him a drink; For in so doing you will heap coals of fire on his head." Do not be overcome by evil, but overcome evil with good (Rom. 12:17-21).

Did you read that? You are to live at peace as much as it depends on you. You are responsible for your actions, attitude, thoughts, words, doing good in the sight of all men, and serving your enemy. It's all about your willing heart to honor and glorify God. If you're not sure how your difficult person feels loved then ask, "What can I do to show you that I love you?" or "How can I be of service to you today?" Make it fun and lighthearted saying that you want to make sure they feel loved. When you feel unloved give a gentle reminder by saying what you want, "I need a hug from you." or "I want to spend time with you."

Remember to check-in to ask, "Have you felt loved by me lately?" Start overcoming evil with blessing and watch what happens.

Praise you, merciful Father full of grace. Thank you for not repaying me evil with evil, but instead you blessed me by sending your Son to die for me. Thank you for your Spirit that empowers me with love, joy, peace, patience, kindness, goodness, faithfulness, gentleness, and self-control. Help me to bless _____ with prayer, speaking the truth in love, sharing my testimony, spending time together, giving hugs, gifts, and serving him/her. Thank you that when I sow to please the Spirit I reap eternal life, instead of pleasing my sinful nature that leads to destruction. I praise you that I can overcome the enemy by the blood of the Lamb and by the word of my testimony. When people insult, persecute, and falsely say all kinds of evil against me because of you, I will rejoice and be glad because my reward is great in heaven. For it is yours to avenge, you will repay evil. With my freedom in Christ, I choose to serve in love instead of indulge my sinful nature, to bring you all honor, glory, and praise. In Jesus' name I pray. Amen.
1 Peter 3:9; Gal. 5:16-23; Galatians 6:8; Revelation 12:11; Matthew 5:3-12; Romans 12:19; Galatians 5:13.

GOD'S TRANSFORMING TRUTH
Overcome evil with blessing to receive a blessing: "Do not repay evil with evil or insult with insult, but with blessing, because to this you were called so that you may inherit a blessing." (1 Peter 3:9)

QUESTION TO PONDER
How can you bless the unlovable person in your life?

TAKE ACTION
Ask the difficult person, "How do you feel most loved?" Discuss what you've learned in this chapter.

Chapter Seven

Wise-Up to Understand

If any of you lacks wisdom, you should ask God, who
gives generously to all without finding fault, and it will
be given to you. But when he asks,
he must believe and not doubt.
James 1:5-6

Rejected people can feel unlovable and worthless. People can be cruel. Labels and put-downs can play back in our mind over and over again until we believe the lie, which can become a self-fulfilling prophecy. For Janine, that's exactly what happened.

Janine's Testimony

Janine was abandoned by her mother. One day her mother dropped her off at kindergarten, proceeded to divorce her father, and moved away without saying goodbye. Janine experienced shame from the rejection of her mother and the humiliation of not having a mother in her life. Janine lived at her grandparent's home where her grandfather molested her, as he had done to his own children. Her handsome young father and his brothers, who had been sexually abused, used sex, drugs, and alcohol to cover up their pain. The family had a bad reputation in town. By association Janine adopted the negative labels the family carried, feeling judged by the teachers as well as parents of classmates who had prohibited their children from playing with her.

As an adult, the painful abandonment of her mother, the sexual immorality committed against her, and the choices she made to be promiscuous as a young adult caused Janine to loathe herself. When we met she had little trust for women. One day I showed up at her house to drop something off for Bible study. At the time, she was agonizing over her past and crying out to God. She invited me into her home convinced that God had brought me to her. Janine had recently accepted Jesus into her heart and for the first time she shared her painful past with me. Without judgment I listened and prayed for Jesus to deliver her of the disturbing nightmares she had endured for years as well as for Him to comfort, heal, and restore her life.

Miraculously, Janine's daunting nightmares vanished and through her study of the Bible she gained self-worth. For the first time, Janine saw the pain of her mother's childhood and the guilt of her mother's decision to abandon her daughter that had plagued their distant relationship over the years. She forgave her mother who had remarried and formed a new family that rarely included her. Instead of looking at her own pain, Janine began to understand her mother. This led to acceptance and healing, which allowed Janine to begin a new legacy of being fully devoted to her husband and children.

Wise-Up to Understand Pain

Is your difficult person hurt from his or her past, maybe a childhood pain or the pain from a previous relationship? Our history with that person or a past relationship or how we were raised can impact the way in which we interact with people. Often we respond out of woundedness. If possible, determine to understand why the person is upset. This may not diminish *your* pain, but it can give you greater understanding toward that unlovable person, which can lead to compassion and empathy. And somehow with that understanding, the offense done toward us is diminished in light of what they endured.

Not only do we need to take time to wise-up to the story behind other people's behavior, we also need to take time to look at our own behavior and why we do the things we do. In the chapter *Forgive to Be*

Set Free, I taught the steps to forgive. In that process we looked back on those offenses that defined us. Until we heal from those hurts, we react from that pain, and our bitterness has the potential to hurt others, and so on through the generations. We must stop to wise-up, learn, and heal. Recognize that bullying, put downs, and inappropriate labels are not about you, but more likely an outward cry for love from the instigator. Compassion can be our companion toward the abuser instead of becoming offended and reactionary.

One explanation for false accusations or sharp responses can be when people project a significant individual from their past onto a current relationship. This can often be seen in the case of a dysfunctional mother-son relationship where he may expect his wife to act in a certain way or assume that she is going to follow in the same footsteps as his mother causing anxiety and stress that he projects onto his wife. The same can be true with the father-daughter relationship. The daughter may project her father onto her husband. It makes sense, when we recognize that we learn from our role models and past history of what we experienced or what we observed in the interaction of our primary family relationships as with our mother, father, and siblings.

We respond and assume certain roles and behavior according to our experiences and what we were taught. A past relationship can teach us what we subconsciously expect in future relationships. Our expectations can create false assumptions. A simple example of this is how a person who has been betrayed through divorce, by their parents or in a previous marriage, may have trust issues that interfere with their current marriage. When we are aware of the dynamics of our primary relationships in the home growing up and how they affected us, then we can make a conscience effort to not project that person of influence from the past onto a current relationship. In fact, it's vital that we never project our past onto our present. It's not fair. Yes, we learn from our mistakes and the behavior of others, but we can't allow a painful relationship or the decisions that others have made in a prior relationship to influence the way we treat another person. If you're projecting past experiences or someone else's experiences onto another person in your life then stop. Hold your thoughts captive and remind yourself that this person is not the same person. If you are projecting your fears onto another then you are treating them accordingly and will often drive those fears to fulfillment.

When we are sensitive to someone's past we are open to understand certain unlovable responses they may have. Ask questions to discover his or her upbringing or past relationships to determine hidden fears they may project onto you. On the other hand, if he or she will not share for various reasons, imagine what could have happened to demonstrate empathy instead of reacting. As you build trust in the relationship, affirm your love and gently remind them that you are not the same person as they may be projecting upon you.

Janine initially shared intimate details about her painful past fearing that I would be like her other friends who gossiped and betrayed her trust. I assured her that I would never reveal what she shared with me without her prior permission. Over time I gained her confidence as a trusted friend. As she shared with others about her painful past she has learned to trust other women and she no longer projects her past relationships onto her current friendships. In fact, she has been set free of all shame to share her testimony to help others heal from their pain of abuse.

Wise-Up to Understand Perspective

Like most couples, opposites attract. My husband and I were no exception. I festered over our differences in the way we handled raising our children, the way I *thought* he restricted my spending, and how often he wanted sex. On top of that, tension mounted between Mark and me when Connor was diagnosed with leukemia. In fact, a social worker at Children's Hospital met with us before Connor's bone marrow transplant to tell us to do everything we could to get along, since additional stress on Connor could cause complications.

Later we discovered that men and women often handle crises differently. Mark wanted to spend every moment with Connor, which I appreciated but failed to communicate at the time. On the other hand, I embraced friends who came to visit us in the hospital. To my husband it appeared that I was more interested in having a party than tending to our son. Trying to be hospitable in that difficult setting, I was eager to share with our visitors the miracles God was doing. I was positive and trusting God, also aware of my example to friends and family during this trial, but my husband misunderstood it. And his condemning thoughts told me so. We both felt rejected.

Often we misinterpret information and people's intentions. In the insightful book *Difficult Conversations* the authors suggest being curious about what happened instead of being certain that you already know. Often it's best to assume the position of ignorance and ask questions instead of assume the person meant to hurt you. Before you react, ask, what just happened? Instead of thinking the person is irrational and incompetent go into discovery mode to probe for information.[7]

Use Jesus as a role model to slow down to hear the stories of people. He was interested in knowing how they felt, how they were suffering, and why they came to see Him. He understood their needs and He met those needs. He showed compassion on a large crowd and healed their sick and fed them. He had compassion on the blind, the lame, the demon possessed, those in bondage of sin and shame, and those who had lost loved ones. He asks us to have compassion on hurting people. When we remember that hurting people act out in unlovable ways then it makes it easier to understand their viewpoint.

We each make sense of what happened from our perspective with the information we assess. We notice words and situations differently, and we have different backgrounds and experiences that influence how we handle conflict. We need not think that our viewpoint is right or better, but in humility accept that there are many ways to look at a situation or a problem. God says, *"When pride comes then comes disgrace, but with humility comes wisdom" (Proverbs 11:2)*. Pride is sneaky. It says my way is the best way. I'm right and you're wrong. I'm better or I deserve better or I'm entitled. It's all about me, me, me.

Remember, as Christians, we must be wise in how we deal with our relationships. Satan, the enemy of this world, wants to deceive, destroy, and distract us from God. He is most successful at doing this by causing confusion, chaos, and misunderstandings in our relationships. The Bible says,

> *Be very careful, then, how you live—not as unwise but as wise, making the most of every opportunity, because the days are evil (Ephesians 5:15-16).*

Be aware that the enemy wants to deceive you. Understand that your purpose is to minister love, grace, and mercy to the hearts of hurting people. Take every opportunity to be wise and not foolish in the words that you say. To argue is foolishness and pride. Does that mean you agree with everyone? No, of course not. Stop to listen, process what they say, and without defensiveness ask questions to clarify so that you can meet their need to be heard and to be known.

Taking the time to ask questions and pay attention to what is said will communicate that you care. Decide to learn. Wise-up to the following areas, although it may appear insignificant, it can change your relationship:

> ➢ Favorite foods, books, movies, and TV shows
> ➢ Work, school, projects, friends, sports, and the players
> ➢ Best memories or most challenging times

Approach every conversation or confrontation with the intent to gain understanding into what makes them unique. Express appreciation for their thoughts, opinions, and feelings. We all want to be known and valued. We long for adoration, affirmation, and acceptance by people in our homes, businesses, and in our communities. And this is true of unlovable people. When we realize their need to be known we can slow down to hear their heart and appreciate their likes and dislikes. To gain insight into the difficult person's daily life will transform the relationship. Ask open ended questions such as:

> ➢ What are your plans for today?
> ➢ What do you like about your friend?
> ➢ If you could do anything this weekend what would you do?

> ➤ Do you feel nurtured by being indoors or outside in nature?
> ➤ Do you get energized with people or spending time alone?

Ask questions to learn, but don't stop there. Remember what she tells you. Follow up with a question about the test in Algebra or the meeting at work or by making her favorite meal or suggest watching his favorite show, or know the score of the football game. It's taking the time to listen and learn that will transform your relationship. If you ask personal questions and people are reluctant to share don't get defensive. Be aware that they may have trust issues and fear of condemnation, judgment, gossip, retaliation, or even harm depending on their past relationships. To establish openness we need to be trusted. Our motivation must come from a pure heart and a place of genuine interest. When your heart is right, ask questions to discover and explore. You will be amazed at what you find out.

Perspective on Nurture

Understanding the way people are wired differently will help us respond appropriately without unrealistic expectations. Instead of becoming frustrated that Mark is different than me I can embrace our differences and find them comical at times. For instance, I'm nurtured by creation and being outside. I enjoy my backyard. When I see a hummingbird or a flower or a butterfly it feels like a kiss from God. Nature reflects a bit of heaven to me. For Mark, when he comes into the backyard he will immediately notice the poop on the grass instead of the flowers. We laugh about it now.

Although Mark is nurtured by being inside and would rather sit in the comfort of a cool home, to please me he will sit outside on a cool morning. Mark especially doesn't like eating outside due to the bugs harassing his food, yet he knows that I enjoy it. Occasionally we eat outside and when we do, the flies or bees immediately come after *his* food. Now we find the humor in the situation instead of feeling frustrated and annoyed with one another.

Perspective on Finances

With finances try to understand where the person is coming from when they react. They will often have more information than we do or they have projected what might take place. For example, the person in your family that takes care of the finances will be aware of the expenses that are coming due. This person may react to overspending more than the person who is not paying the bills. When I came in with shopping bags I immediately put my husband on the defensive. His look of disapproval used to aggravate me and I would justify my spending by telling him I saved money, since the items were on sale. This never worked well! He would respond, "You can't save money when you spend it." Some people are spenders and others are savers. It's important to establish goals on how to handle finances to feel safe in the relationship, which will be addressed in the next chapter.

Perspective on Words and Facial Expressions

Our words and facial expressions can mean different things. Some people are unaware of what they do and what it implies. When I started asking my husband why he rolled his eyes when I said something, at times he had no idea he was doing it. I explained how it made me feel discounted and he apologized. Over time he was able to stop this habit as I *gently* reminded him when he did it. Notice the emphasis on the word *gently*.

Often what we say is not really what we mean. Some people are "word" people. They listen and analyze what is said or implied. For example, when I said to my husband, *we* need to clean the BBQ, I was really asking, *Will you clean the BBQ?* This caused conflict with my husband who felt manipulated. Wising-up, I began to be more direct, asking him if he would please do the chore. My directness is well received by my analytical husband who would rather not beat around the bush, but instead, have me say what's on my mind and what I want. This is why clarifying what a person means is essential to good communication.

Perspective on Mental Illness

Before moving on, I want to briefly address the issue of mental illness and how it relates to becoming wise in dealing with people who are suffering in this way. The person affected with emotional and mental disorders, depression, and phobias contribute to unhealthy behavior caused by a distorted worldview. Remember that the person is not intentionally trying to hurt you or be difficult, but that the illness is compelling them to act in an unlovable way. Often they try their best to cope with the illness and we can show them grace. Understanding their mental challenges can help alleviate the tendency to take their behavior personally.

We must do our best to understand where the person is coming from and to recognize their limitations. When we understand their past pain, perspectives, and personality we can make sense of the conflict, demonstrate empathy, and make appropriate decisions for the relationship. The following chapters will teach more biblical truths on how to love difficult people without enabling them. It is possible that with all our efforts to understand, we may not come to a satisfying conclusion or reason for their behavior, but we can show love even when we do not fully understand their perspective. Loving beyond our own understanding is God's love demonstrated through us.

Wise-Up to Understand Personalities

A part of our growth is to understand how we are different from others and to accept and appreciate those differences. At first opposites attract, but later those very traits can drive us crazy. Wisdom can be gained when we engage in conversations to seek understanding of our own growth opportunities. Encourage the difficult person to be honest with you about how you can change. Assure him or her that you will not become angry. The purpose is to understand how you're wired with different personalities to come together to accomplish great things. We need one another. If we were all the same we would be limited to what we can do. I always say that my kids would be messed up if it were just me raising them or just my husband. We both contribute to their growth with our different personalities. Although we have our weaknesses, we have our strengths to balance one another.

There are four basic personality types to keep in mind when dealing with people. Most will overlap into two of the four categories. To keep it simple I will refer to the primary social styles, which include the Amiable, Analytical, Driver, and Expressive. Conflict often arises when dealing with different personality types than your own. Here's a quick overview to help you understand the benefits and opportunities of each personality type:

Amiable Personality

- Kind-hearted, may avoid conflict at the expense of being honest in expressing their wants and needs
- Easily transition into new environments
- May appear wishy-washy when unable to make firm decisions
- Sensitive, empathetic, soft-spoken and eager to please

Analytical Personality

- Detail oriented people and extremely perceptive
- Usually need all the facts to make a decision
- Often make great accountants and engineers
- Analyzing people and circumstances can appear critical and pessimistic

Driver Personality

- Task and objective-focused with high energy
- Know what they want and how to get there
- Communicate facts quickly and to the point
- Can appear insensitive to the people around them
- May do what it takes to get the results whatever the cost
- Hardworking and confident with conflict

Expressive Personality

- Natural salesperson and story-teller
- Warm, enthusiastic, and engaging
- Good motivator, encourager, and communicator

- Can dominate conversations, can be insensitive to others who are quieter
- Can tend to exaggerate, leaving valuable facts or details out
- Sometimes can talk about things rather than do them

Naturally, when we familiarize ourselves with the different personalities, greater understanding and less judgment can be achieved. Realize that there is probably no intention on the part of the unlovable person to annoy or cause dissention. Their behavior is merely influenced by the way God created them, no better or worse than you. In fact, we need each other. By understanding our differences we can rejoice in our strengths and show grace in our weaknesses. Personality experts Dr. Robert and Dorothy Bolton share ways to adapt.[8]

Adapt to the Amiable

Avoid intensity and harshness. Be gentle. Ask questions to explore their opinions. Slow down to listen carefully and seek to understand without judgment or condemnation. Do not attempt to manipulate, control, or counter them with logic. Encourage expression of any reservations, fears, or questions. Without pressure or intimidation, decide on goals, negotiate an action plan with deadlines, and follow through on responsibilities.

Adapt to the Analytical

Avoid small talk. Quickly get down to business by being prepared, logical, and giving facts. Show benefits with pros and cons of proposed goals focusing on minimal risk. Analytics are turned off by exaggerations of the advantages. Action-plan must be clear with milestone dates and progress reports scheduled.

Adapt to the Driver

Be on time, energetic, and fast paced with direct eye contact. Be honest, precise, and organized without over-explaining. Present the key facts and use them logically and quickly staying focused on the topic to honor time limits.

Adapt to the Expressive

Be intentional with direct eye contact. Allow time for socializing to discover their dreams. Talk about experiences, opinions, and people by using stories to make a point. Focus on the overall goal or idea and then present action plans. Be energetic and fun while achieving the objective.

Extrovert verses Introvert

Not only has God wired us with different personalities, but also within those four personality types we are wired in two different ways to obtain our energy. Determine if you're wired as an extrovert or introvert. Wise-up to how you get your energy. Pay attention to how the person you're in conflict with gets their energy. Be sensitive to the way you each are wired. Allow space for them to spend time with other people or by themselves, in order to be refueled.

For me, when I humbled myself to gain insight into the way my husband is wired our relationship improved from frustration to appreciation. My husband works hard in the office during the week, surrounded by people and going from one meeting to another. The environment is intense and stressful. Although he loves it, I have come to understand that when Mark gets home from work he needs down time. He enjoys relaxing on the couch in front of the TV or on the computer in the evenings to gain energy.

An introvert can be very social, but she or he is energized by time alone. Introverts can be the life of the party, but at the end of the party they are drained for days. Often the introvert can be reserved, but what they do say is very insightful. The introvert enjoys curling up with a good book or needs their computer or video time. She can stay behind the scenes not vying for attention like the extrovert.

Most extroverts can suck the energy out of the introvert. They are energized when they are with people. Alone for a period of time, they are drained of all their energy. As an extrovert I feel rejuvenated with people. When my children were young I made a point of getting together with other moms at the park so my kids could play and I could socialize. Throughout the years there have been times that I made the local coffee shop a place to get energized each morning. Not only did the caffeine help, but the friendly people gave me a buzz for the day. This was a place where I felt seen and known as they remembered my name and my favorite drink.

Introverts, keep in mind that when you make plans to spend time with an extrovert you may feel abandoned when the extrovert begins giving attention to other people around you. Recognize that the extrovert is not intentionally neglecting you, but has the attitude "the more the merrier." If this behavior bothers you, calmly explain what you want by saying, "I look forward to our time together. Can we go where our focus can be on one another instead of being interrupted by people you know?" If you're an extrovert be sensitive to who you engage with when you are scheduled to spend quality time with an introvert.

Task verses Relationship

We have two modes of operation: task and relationship. Our task mode is focused on accomplishing a project, task, or problem at hand. This task can take on many forms such as paying bills, preparing dinner, updating social media status, responding to emails, relaxing to rejuvenate, reading the news, studying, or helping kids with homework. Whenever we are trying to concentrate we are in task mode. We potentially can become frustrated and annoyed when we are interrupted.

Relationship mode is full concentration on the person in front of you. Nothing else matters but that relationship. For some people, we are more driven by relationships. We actually avoid doing tasks or become easily distracted from the task when there is someone in need of our time. When we recognize that there are two separate modes we can understand people and be sensitive to which mode of operation they are in at the moment. For example, when I see my husband working at the computer I can ask him "Are you doing a task?" If he answers yes, then I can say, "When do you have time for our relationship?" Usually he responds by saying how much time he needs to complete his task. Once completed, he can be fully focused on me.

Understanding task mode and relationship mode has helped to transform many relationships. Previously, a woman named Delores had resented her children when they interrupted her, wanting her attention when she was on the phone or making dinner. Out of frustration she snapped at them until she recognized that she was in the middle of a task. Instead of her children getting their feelings hurt or becoming defensive, she reminded them calmly that she was in task mode and would be available to spend time with them after her task was completed.

For many people today, the computer or cell phone can be a source of contention. Interrupting someone who is in the middle of emailing or texting may cause them to be curt with you or ignore you all together. When this happens, if you have already identified the phrase "task mode" and "relationship mode" then gently ask, "Are you upset with me because I interrupted your task?" Agree that by using the words "task" or "relationship" you will both stop to recognize your response of agitation and restore the relationship with an apology. Often we need to finish our task to switch gears to be in relationship. Identify the pain of rejection to communicate it with grace, understanding their response is probably not about you, but finishing the task.

Planner verses Spontaneous

Some are planners and some are spontaneous. Once the spontaneous person understands that conflict can be alleviated simply by making a plan, your relationship can change. The planner usually needs a plan to function without stress. The spontaneous can cause a great deal of stress when she is at the last minute requesting demands from everyone due to her lack of planning. On the other hand, she shows respect for the planner when she thinks ahead to plan, be organized, and follow through on her commitments.

Whether you're a planner or spontaneous you must learn to be flexible and considerate. Without a plan you will surely fail. The planner can be a beneficial partner for the spontaneous person. In the same way, the spontaneous will offer excitement and opportunities that the planner may never experience without the spontaneous person in their life. The key to all our differences is to demonstrate wisdom by taking the time to learn about one another in the areas of the three P's: Pain, Perspective, and Personality.

Wise-Up through Prayer

Pandemonium permeated my home. The other three children were lashing out in anger, jealous of the time we spent with Connor in the hospital, gripped by fear of what might happen to our family. Desperate, I fell to my knees, often crying out to God during the yearlong treatment. It was in these moments alone with God that I felt His loving arms embrace me and lift me up. I discovered His overwhelming comfort and peace in my time of trouble.

Near the end of Connor's one hundred days of isolation and after his bone marrow transplant, I considered separation from my husband. Emotionally we were already separated. I had pulled away from his angry outbursts and accusations instead of gently confronting him. It was important that I seek God wholeheartedly before making the choice to officially separate. In my quiet time I had prayed, *"Search me, O God, and know my heart; test me and know my anxious thoughts. See if there is any offensive way in me, and lead me in the way everlasting" (Psalm 139:23-24).* Watch out when you pray that prayer! God will start taking off the blinders to the sin you once justified. That sin will become obvious and even repulsive. God began to show me my wicked ways. Over the years He gently convicted me of my sins one by one, not all at once, but gradually as a gracious father does.

At this time, God showed me how I slandered my husband's reputation. He revealed truth to me through the Bible as I asked him to speak to me when I opened His Word. Reading Proverbs 12:4 convicted my heart, *"A wife of noble character is her husband's crown, but a disgraceful wife is like decay in his bones."* God showed me that I needed to honor my husband by not sharing every detail of what he did or said with every person who asked me how Connor was doing during his treatment. Of course, I had justified my slander by doing it in the name of prayer.

Brokenhearted and crushed, God was asking me to obey His Word. Shortly after reading the words in the Bible, while driving to a Women's Retreat with my friends, I noticed a flutter in my ear as I began to say something negative about my husband. Stunned, I stopped to consider that this was a sign from the Holy Spirit, a reminder to not gossip. Immediately, I asked God to forgive me. Later during the weekend, I sat with a woman who offered to pray with me. I began to share about my husband in more detail than was necessary when the flutter happened again. Aware that God was talking to me, I shut my mouth quickly to honor God and my husband.

On the weekend of the Women's Retreat God orchestrated divine appointments. In small groups women shared their struggles. Many who had persevered in their marriages had found healing. Those who were divorced were still dealing with ex-spouses and irresponsible dads. The women who remarried were struggling with their blended families caused by different parenting values. Because of this insight my heart was convicted that it would be better to work on my marriage with my children under my care and custody than to deal with the complications of divorce.

Wisdom is found when we ask God with a humble and believing heart. In James 1:5-6, God says, *"If any of you lacks wisdom, you should ask God, who gives generously to all without finding fault, and it will be given to you. But when he asks, he must believe and not doubt."* Ask God to show you the truth. He is always faithful. His wisdom comes in different ways. Sometimes God uses our friends and family to convey wisdom, but be careful. Use discernment to align their message with God's Word as you seek Him in prayer. God can use difficult people to speak words of truth and wisdom when we humble ourselves to listen.

Maturity is demonstrated when we are able to evaluate a conflict and respond without annoyance, irritation, or frustration. Patience is a sure sign of wisdom as promised in the Proverbs, *"A person's wisdom yields patience; it is to one's glory to overlook an offense"*

(Proverbs 19:11). With wisdom comes patience to overlook jabs and spears that people throw, understanding that the person comes from a place of pain. Although we have feelings that we should not deny, with wisdom we can identify the feeling and decide whether we say anything. Stop to pray about your response before you say it. Wisdom considers the future consequences of our words, choosing with the best intentions that which will bring about peace. A wise person will listen intently; clarify what he heard with appreciation of that person's thoughts, opinions, and feelings. He communicates respect with body language as he crafts his words carefully with gentleness.

To hear what someone is saying will give us the opportunity to grow in love and righteousness. This wasn't always easy for me, but when I practiced what I preached God rewarded me. For example, when my husband and children complained about me being on the computer all the time, I was defensive. I justified the endless hours of writing, since I was accomplishing my goal to help others. In my effort to help people, I sacrificed my most important relationships. I realized conflict was a cry for attention. My family felt neglected by me. I needed to change something to accomplish my goals.

Through prayer God revealed ways I could change. My desk is situated with my back toward the family in the living area. Instead of ignoring them, most of the time, I get up from my desk to acknowledge them in an attempt to make them feel special and adored by me, to see them, and learn about them. When they watch a movie, there are times I will pick up my laptop and join them on the sofa. But often I turn off the computer to be involved in what they do, even watching a program I might not be interested in. Now I attempt to get most of my work done during the day when children are at school and my husband is at work. Since doing this simple gesture my family relationships have improved. I communicated that they are more important than my work or ministry.

Actions speak louder than words so demonstrate that you love that person who is acting out. Instead of withdrawing, pursue the relationship to discover who they are. There will always be people in this world that *need* you. In fact, I found that I gravitated toward people to feel significant, affirmed, and accepted. As I sacrificed the praise of others to see, know, and hear my own family, I communicated that they were significant. As a result, I found love in my own home.

Wise Father, I praise you for your divine wisdom that you give generously without finding fault when I ask. Help me to gain wisdom to understand the pain, perspective, and personality of _____ so that I may respond appropriately. Forgive me of my pride that produces disgrace and allow me to always be humble to acquire wisdom. Through the grace and power of Christ in me I pray that I can listen effectively by holding my tongue. Help me to not overreact with hurt feelings, which will lead to defensiveness, lashing out in anger, and self-righteousness. Search me, O God, and know my heart; test me and know my anxious thoughts. See if there is any offensive way in me, and lead me in the way everlasting. Let me bring glory to you as wisdom yields patience and I am able to overlook an offense. Give me wisdom in understanding the pain that has been inflicted on _____ by me and others. Show me his/her perspective that I might see things more clearly. Help me to rejoice in the way that you created his/her personality so that we can benefit one another for your glory and praise. In Jesus' name I pray. Amen.
James 1:5-6; Proverbs 11:2; Psalm 139:23-24; Proverbs 19:11.

GOD'S TRANSFORMING TRUTH
Ask God for wisdom who gives generously: "If any of you lacks wisdom, you should ask God, who gives generously to all without finding fault, and it will be given to you. But when he asks, he must believe and not doubt." (James 1:5-6)

QUESTION TO PONDER
What past painful relationships, perspectives, and personality traits are impacting your difficult relationship?

TAKE ACTION
Be vulnerable. Share your past pain, perspectives, and personality with transparency to build trust. Ask questions to know and understand the hurt person.

Chapter Eight

Establish the Goal to Protect

Love always protects.
1 Corinthians 13:7

Unless we clearly define goals, our needs go unmet. This is true in our workplace, home, church, or community. Often responsibilities are communicated at work, in our service to the church and community, but we neglect to talk about our responsibilities in our relationships closest to home. Naturally we desire and strive to have peace in our lives, yet we surrender to mediocrity and settle for unrest. Through years of turmoil, misunderstandings, and ups and downs in our marriage, my husband and I finally discovered that our biggest problem was that we failed to establish the goal to protect one another and our family. Together we created some general house rules to feel safe.

God created rules to protect us. His rules are communicated through the Bible, often referred to as the Law or the Ten Commandments. These rules or guidelines are not to restrict our freedom but to give us freedom from guilt and shame and consequences. Biblical guidelines give us tools on how to love God, ourselves, and others. Laws in the United States protect one another from being hurt. God longs for all people to feel safe. We are all created equal in the image of God; therefore, we must value and respect all life. When we stand for righteousness for all people then we remain in a right relationship with God and with the people in our lives. In the definition of love the Bible says, *"Love always protects" (1 Cor. 13:7).*

135

All human life must feel safe and secure regardless of age, race, gender, or religious beliefs. Life is precious and must be protected against evil.

Some people might look at the Commandments and determine that it's all about what not to do, while these rules actually help us better understand what to do. These guidelines seem lofty and unattainable, but God still wants us to try. And it's only with His help that we can follow them. Our sinful nature wants to rebel and that's precisely why Jesus came. The Bible says that to break the Old Testament Law we deserve death, but instead we have a loving and righteous God who came to pay our penalty of eternal death to give us everlasting life with Him. Here's a reminder of God's rules from Matthew 22:37-39 and Exodus 20:1-17, which I adapted into a positive list of guidelines to achieve peace and harmony in our difficult relationships:

God Established Rules to Protect You

1. Love the Lord your God with all of your heart, your mind, your soul, and your strength. And the second is like it: Love your neighbor as yourself.
2. Put your relationship with God first before people, careers, material possessions or anything else. After God your primary relationships should be your spouse, then your children, your biological and church family members, and others in the workplace and community.
3. Use God's name only to bring Him honor, glory, and praise.
4. Commit to learning about God, worshipping, and following Him every day. Let there be a day of rest where you put all other things aside to focus on Him.
5. Honor and respect your father and your mother, so that you may enjoy a long and prosperous life.
6. Be loving and kind without becoming easily angered so not to commit murder in your heart.
7. Look at men and women with respect and honor so as to not commit adultery by lusting after him or her.

8.   Work as unto the Lord. Be generous without taking money that belongs to others which can include cheating on taxes, copying music, not using work-time appropriately.
9.   Tell the truth always in love, there's no such thing as a white lie. Let your yes be yes and your no be no to say what you want and what you expect.
10.   Be satisfied with your possessions and your spouse without lusting after what others have.

Many people have a wrong concept of God. They believe God to be angry, distant, restrictive, demanding perfection, and insensitive to our desires to have fun. But the opposite is true of God. He is overwhelmed with love for us. Due to His great love He desires to give us guidelines to protect us. These guidelines help us to have peace and a joy-filled life without regrets. And when we stumble and fall God picks us up and forgives us.

The Goal to Protect Yourself

To protect yourself you must respect yourself. Do you honor your mind, body, and spirit? If you don't, no one will. How do you allow people to treat you? Determine to stand-up to value yourself so that others will value you. In my opinion, the lack of respect we have towards ourselves is due to a lack of understanding of who God created us to be. Instead of finding our self-worth as a reflection of our Creator, beautifully knit together in the image of God and a temple of the Holy Spirit with divine purpose, we believe the lies that people tell us. Destructive and demeaning words – like, *you're worthless or stupid, you'll never amount to anything,* or the message *you evolved from an ape* – plague our society with an egocentric, barbaric mentality to gratify the lusts of our flesh and selfish ambitions at the expense of honoring human life. Without valuing ourselves we cave into the demands of others instead of protecting the precious person we were created to be. Do you understand your worth in the sight of God? Jesus demonstrated the Father's love when He died for you. For that reason, you should protect yourself and teach others to do the same in the following areas:

Mind: Guard your mind by being selective as to what you watch, the books you read, and the internet sites you look at. Beware of the music you listen to and the words you and others speak. Avoid alcohol, drugs, and substances that can distort your thinking. Fill your mind with good and wholesome information that will keep you focused on God and His plans for you. Memorize the Word of God to think on what is right, true, excellent, and praiseworthy.

Body: Protect your body from harm. Care for your physical body with proper rest, nutrition, water, and exercise. Your body is a temple of the living God through the indwelling of the Holy Spirit through a relationship with Jesus. Your body must function properly to be used by God to minister to His people effectively.

Spirit: Protect your heart and soul by waking up early to spend time with Jesus. Praise and worship the Lord who is your strength, refuge, and hope. Read and meditate on the Word of God to be nourished, gain wisdom, and protect yourself from the lies of the enemy. Be in constant communication with your Creator throughout your day calling on the name of Jesus. Obey God's Word in order to be blessed with the fruit of the Spirit and to see Him at work in your life.

Obviously, we can't live in a bubble. We are to live in the world, but not be of the world (John 17:14). The enemy is clever to hold us captive to this world through the energizing beat of music, seductive and violent movies, and the allure of media and books to play with our insecurities that make us something we were never supposed to be. Lies interconnect illicit sex as making love, drugs and alcohol as having fun, and the lust for more as satisfying the desires of the soul. The truth is that we are left empty, lonely, and broken as we try to fill the God-shaped void that our heavenly Father created in us for a relationship that only Jesus can satisfy.

Sexual immorality destroys true intimacy and distorts our identity. Later in life this seems to contribute to the high number of those who suffer from depression, low self-worth, and conflict in relationships. In the book *Hooked,* authors Dr. Joe McIlhaney and Dr. Freda McKissic-Bush, share startling research on the breakthroughs of sexuality on the development of the brain in adolescents and young adults. Discoveries show that the pattern of multiple sexual partners creates a neurological change in the brain that prevents a healthy relational bond from occurring later in a committed marriage.[9]

Society tells us *if it feels good do it,* but God tells us that we are valuable and precious and not to give away what is sacred and special. Failure to protect and value your own life is also a sin against God who dwells within you through the Holy Spirit when you have a relationship with Jesus. God has entrusted you to honor and respect your body, which includes taking care of yourself physically, emotionally, mentally, and spiritually. The Bible warns,

> *Flee from sexual immorality. All other sins a man commits are outside his body, but he who sins sexually sins against his own body. Do you not know that your body is a temple of the Holy Spirit, who is in you, whom you have received from God? You are not your own; you were bought at a price. Therefore honor God with your body (1 Cor. 6:18-20).*

You were bought with the blood of Jesus. He paid for you to live a life of freedom from immorality. He put His Spirit in you for you to live by the Spirit and for the Spirit and with the Spirit. A lack of self-respect toward yourself not only impacts your own self-worth, but injures the person whom you allow to treat you poorly. Sin separates you from a holy God as well as the people you sin against. If you allow someone to sin against you then you contribute to that person being separated from not only you, but from God. You cause them to stumble, which brings despair, destruction, and spiritual death.

139

The Goal to Protect Your Spouse

We have a God of order. He illustrates this through the intricacy of His creation that is aligned perfectly as the earth is just the right distance from the sun so we neither freeze nor burn up in flames. Organisms carry genetic information constructing complex DNA to bring beauty and purpose to creation. The Holy Scriptures demonstrate divine order in the way they are consistent from the beginning of Genesis to the end of Revelation speaking the truth of God's love and mercy for all people and judgment on those who reject and hate Him.

Just as God has created order in the physical world, God has created order to function properly as a society. In the United States we have a President with a Vice President under him and a Congress, a Senate, and a judicial system that perform responsibilities to the state and local levels. The same is true in companies, organizations, churches, and families. There is a chain of command or authority in the decision making process. Too often conflict comes when we fail to define the roles of our relationship.

There are unspoken guidelines established in a marriage covenant that communicate respect for a spouse. Husbands and wives are to honor and submit to one another. My own marriage improved dramatically as we made a plan on how to function in our roles. We determined that my husband needed to be the leader of our home as God designed the family to have one head of household. I decided to support him instead of undermine his authority, to let him be responsible to lead our family spiritually, and ultimately to make the final decision when we were at a standstill. We agreed to talk about the options when it came to purchasing items, disciplining the kids, visiting in-laws, serving outside the home, planning activities, and being sexually intimate. Allowing our husbands to be the leaders of our home often encourages them to step up to take on that responsibility. As wives we can say to them,

"You are the leader of our home. You have been chosen by God to lead our family in how to love God as well as to love, respect, and serve others. I want to follow you and encourage our children to follow your example. Of course, I don't expect you to be perfect. We all fall short of the glory of God and I accept you as a work in progress, just like I am. I want to come alongside you to help you protect our family. It's our job to protect our children physically, mentally, emotionally, and spiritually."

Whether your husband wants to be the spiritual leader or not, it is his responsibility. As his wife or ex-wife, acknowledge that you will support and encourage him to lead his children. Show compassion and grace when he fails. Show him you are on his side. Ask him how you can help him in his area of weakness. It's easy to demonstrate disappointment and pull-away. In fact, many couples use sexual intimacy as a consequence. Withholding from our spouse due to a lack of interest, as a means to control, or as a way to punish is unhealthy for the relationship. Instead we must address the problem immediately to bring reconciliation. There may be a period of healing that must come if trust has been sacrificed with infidelity. As a rule, remember you alone fulfill sexual intimacy for your spouse. God designed us to long for one another to become one in body, mind, and spirit. We must not allow anyone to separate us from our beloved. Jesus said the following about being united through the covenant of marriage,

At the beginning of creation God made them male and female. 'For this reason a man will leave his father and mother and be united to his wife, and the two will become one flesh.' So they are no longer two, but one flesh. Therefore what God has joined together, let no one separate (Mark 10:6-9).

Many things can separate us from what God joined together as one in marriage. Prior sexual relations and looking at porn can impact our thoughts during intimacy. For this reason, God wants us to honor and respect our body and minds with sexual purity in and out of marriage. Sexual purity *in* marriage is about unselfish motivation, cherishing and appreciating our spouse, speaking truth in love, and engaging in pure thoughts during sexual intimacy. We commit adultery when making love with our spouse if our thoughts are on someone else. In fact, we are not making love with our spouse if we imagine another person. If this is the case with you, confess that sin to God and pray during those times of sexual intimacy to be focused on your beloved.

Furthermore, you may have painful memories of past relationships from sexual abuse or assault. You do not have to allow this horrific experience to interfere with making love to your spouse. It's for this reason that Jesus came to heal you, to take those painful memories away, and bring you abundant life. Seek Him with all of your heart to forgive those who hurt you and to be healed. The topic of forgiveness was addressed in the chapter *Forgive to be Set Free*. Healing will be further addressed in the last chapter *Determine Your Identity*.

If you are more sexually assertive in your marriage, ask if your motivation is out of selfish desires and the lust of the flesh or about pleasing and satisfying the needs of your cherished spouse. We should want to satisfy sexual intimacy with our significant other. This does not mean that you succumb to whatever sexual desires he demands at whatever time. God intended physical intimacy to be based on trust, safety, and protection. When sexual conduct causes potential harm then you can be sure that it's not God's way. Sexual intimacy should never involve coercion, pressure, or guilt to persuade one partner to perform in a manner that is uncomfortable. In the case where someone is uninterested in participating in a sexual act, we must consider if both spouses are feeling honored and protected. For instance, in the case of anal sex there is a high risk of disease. Contact with feces can be like poison in the blood stream and ultimately can lead to infection, disease, and death.

Today many sexually transmitted diseases stem from sexual relations outside the loving covenant of marriage. If a behavior is questionable and you have angst about whether it's right, even if society accepts it, ask yourself *did God intend it to be this way?* If the behavior is unnatural, uncomfortable, or unsafe then communicate your feelings using the guide from the chapter *Express Truth in Love*. God has made it known in our hearts what is right and He clarifies it in His Word. When it comes to sexual intimacy God created man as one of the only species to have sexual intimacy face to face. As we look into the eyes of our beloved spouse, trusting him or her with our heart, we become joined together as one physically, emotionally, and spiritually for life.

Remember to protect your spouse and your marriage by being available to one another. Spend time together. Have fun. And enjoy intimacy. Out of honor and respect for one another, beforehand talk about what will satisfy both your needs. Agree to tell one another when feeling unloved or neglected. Honor one another earlier in the day before making love that night. Decide to give clues with a gentle pat on the butt to be playful and flirtatious. Or create a special word or phrase that says you're interested in making love.

Surrender to one another to ensure that Satan will not destroy the relationship through temptation. God united you with your spouse to be one in spirit, belonging to one another, and yielding your bodies to the other. If there is a reason to be apart for a period of time then commit to lifting your spouse up in prayer to withstand the temptation of infidelity, (1 Cor. 7:4-6).

Remember there is always someone after your spouse. That is the reality of the world we live in. Temptation is everywhere. Many neglected men and women are lured into an extramarital affair because their spouse was unavailable. Society accepts and promotes sexual immorality. In fact, in a popular on-line magazine for men I stumbled across a disturbing article written on how to find a non-clingy mistress. Sad but true, extramarital affairs are common and often accepted by friends, co-workers, and believe it or not, even the betrayed spouse can allow an affair to continue. Don't let this be you. Stand for righteousness! Get some confidence and speak truth in love. Stop the fool from continuing down the path of sexual immorality that will destroy the lives of many.

People having an affair (emotionally or physically) steal time away from work and other commitments. They cannot possibly be attentive to the needs of their family. Instead, they are self-absorbed, resort to lying while they lust after another. Now consider the emotional pain caused to the spouse, the children, parents, extended families, friendships, and future generations. This truth hurts, but healing can happen. We have a God of miracles that can restore a marriage when the betrayed spouse or friends take a stand for righteousness to confront the adulterer with truth spoken in love.

For this reason, do not allow resentment to build a wall between you and your spouse. Get issues resolved quickly. Keep the marriage bed pure. If you feel uninterested, exhausted, and over-worked then wake up to the possibilities of having to do everything on your own as a single parent. Do you want your world torn apart? Do you want to know what it really means to be exhausted and over-committed? Ask any single parent and they will tell you what you need to know. It's hard work!

If your spouse is grumpy and unlovable, he or she may be feeling rejected by you. The lack of sexual intimacy can be the reason for the unlovable behavior. Consider this scenario: you and your spouse decide on the days of the week to make love. Call it "date night" and make it extra special. On those days you mentally prepare for your evening. When your spouse says, "Are you ready for bed?" this is your clue for sexual intimacy. There are no questions running through your mind if he or she will reject you, if he's tired, if she has a headache, or if he's interested. The guessing game is over and the couple is completely ready, willing, and satisfied. Bam!

Dottie's Testimony

Dottie never thought much about the fact that her husband would look at pornography until she became a Christian. When she read the Bible she was convicted of the adultery her husband committed against her. In Matthew 5:28 Jesus says, *"I tell you that anyone who looks at a woman lustfully has already committed adultery with her in his heart."* With Dottie's new understanding, she boldly confronted her husband with a righteous indignation that he was betraying her. He discounted her position; after all, he had engaged in this behavior for ten years of their marriage and she had said nothing.

Standing firm in her boundary, Dottie said something to this effect, "I love you. I belong to you and you belong to me. I am available to you, but I will not tolerate you looking at pornography and if you betray me again in this way then you will have to move out. You will lose the children and me. And I'm serious."

Dottie set a clear boundary and consequence for the sin. Her husband was clear on the rules and what would happen to him if he broke those rules. A couple weeks later she found a movie in the garage. She told her husband that he needed to pack his bags immediately. Her husband promised that the porn was from before and said that he would never again look at pornography. He never realized that he was committing adultery and hurting her.

Due to Dottie establishing firm rules to protect herself and her children, crying out in prayer, putting the computer in their bedroom for her to see what he was looking at during the night, and establishing the consequence that she did, God delivered her husband from his addiction to porn and he became a Christian.

If you are in a situation that involves pornography, consider that the story above is one way to handle this betrayal. Either way, when a sin is committed against you, you must stand up to express boldly what you will tolerate, which will demonstrate respect for yourself and gain respect from your spouse. Often times your confidence will draw your partner toward you. Prayer is essential to be equipped to express God's truth with power, love, and clarity.

You may do *everything* to get the help you need to reconcile an adulterous relationship including humbly surrendering to God, trusting Him, obeying His Word, and seeking Him with all of your heart. The reality is that your spouse may still choose to walk away. Be comforted by God's Word that says after all efforts have been made to reconcile, *"If the unbeliever leaves, let him do so. A believing man or woman is not bound in such circumstances. God has called us to live in peace"* *(1 Cor. 7:15)*. If this is the case, although it may not make sense to you at the time and it may be extremely painful, I ask you to continue to trust God and follow Him. He knows what is best for you and He may be providing you a way out. In the midst of your pain, God will be your Husband, your best friend, and the Lover of your soul, lean in on Him. God promises to restore what the enemy has stolen from you, so that you may praise God who works wonders for you, to never be ashamed again, (Joel 2:25-26).

The Goal to Protect Children

If you have children, grandchildren, nieces, or nephews you have been entrusted to protect them by teaching them God's ways. He says to place the Word in your heart and mind in order to teach them to your children. We are instructed to teach them at breakfast, out and about during the day, and putting them to bed at night (Deut. 11:18-19). We cannot depend on outside sources to teach our children these values. This corrupt world is pulling them away from righteous living and it's up to you to teach them with God's help.

Another way to protect your children, as I already shared, is to fight for your marriage. God created the family to have a father and mother in place, since both contribute to the raising of the children to produce godly offspring. With divorce, single moms or dads are faced with the overwhelming task of providing in all areas of physical, emotional, spiritual, and mental development in their children. Fortunately, there are many amazing single parents who have balanced work as they have raised their children into responsible caring adults in spite of unfortunate circumstances, but it's not easy. Frequently single moms are overworked and underpaid trying to provide financial security for their children if dads are unfaithful to provide support.

Whether married or single, it's important to be physically and emotionally available to your children. Many hurting parents numb the pain of rejection and abuse with sex, drugs, alcohol, overworking, overspending, and focused on other relationships. Rejected children attempt to find attention, affection, and acceptance in the arms of someone who will give it to them. With the breakdown of the family, more and more girls and boys are becoming sexually active. Today many teens expect sexual relations and may use pressure and manipulation to get what they want. Sometimes they repeat the violation that was done to them.

Teach your children how to protect their bodies by saying "no" to alcohol, drugs, and immoral behavior. Warn your children that what God meant as sacred and a beautiful act of intimacy between husband and wife society has warped into something casual, insignificant, and degrading. Discuss how sexual immorality leads to detachment and comparisons that can lead to infidelity and divorce. Do everything you can to protect your children by staying faithful to God and your spouse. Look at God's warning about unfaithfulness:

> Has not the Lord made them one? In flesh and spirit they are His. And why one? Because He was seeking godly offspring. So guard yourself in your spirit, and do not break faith with the wife of your youth. "I hate divorce," says the Lord God of Israel, "and I hate a man's covering himself with violence as well as with his garment," says the Lord Almighty. So guard yourself in your spirit, and do not break faith (Malachi 2:15-16).

Follow and seek after God to guard and protect your spirit, and that of your spouse and children. The family unit is designed to provide a safe, secure, and loving environment to produce well-adjusted, godly children. Of course, evidence is all around us that families fail to achieve this standard. People fail and hurt each other due to their selfish nature. Many times we are left with scars inflicted by others that run deep and lead us down a path of unrighteousness. This is Patty's story.

Patty's Testimony

At the age of ten Patty was molested by her uncle. One night when she sought help from her aunt, the aunt yelled at her husband but never pursued justice. Insecure and lacking confidence, the aunt shrugged off the offense. As a result, Patty's uncle continued molesting many girls including his own daughters and their girlfriends. This man ruined lives and his wife ignored the crimes being committed.

Years later, Patty brought her shame and pain into the light. No longer afraid of her secret, she confronted her aunt who was no longer married to the same man. Her aunt admitted her responsibility and apologized for the trauma she was part of. As they talked openly Patty learned that her aunt had been molested in her youth. Incapable of standing up to her abuser as a young girl, her aunt was also unable to stand up to her abusive husband to protect her own daughters. She lived in fear, believing the twisted lies that her husband would seek revenge and hurt her and her daughters, yet all the while she allowed them and others to be hurt by him sexually.

Patty extended forgiveness to her aunt, but discovered that her sexual abuse came out in her future marriage through her bitterness and her need to prove herself sexually worthy through infidelity. After committing adultery Patty chose to end her marriage and marry another man. When her ex-husband married another woman, Patty admits she became bitter and angry toward the woman who was involved in raising her children. She never reached out to her husband's new wife or said anything encouraging about her to the children. Her bitter, critical spirit and disapproval had a deep and lasting effect on her children. Both Patty and her ex-husband, who was also extremely angry over the divorce, caused their children extreme anxiety with their self-centered behavior and lack of understanding.

Today Patty has many regrets over the hurt she caused her children from her divorce. Her advice to others is to contemplate the long-term ramifications of what divorce means not only to you and your spouse, but to the children. She admits that divorce is very painful for everyone involved. Expect that your spouse is going to find a new partner. Be prepared to share your children with that person. Patty says it's never too late to build a friendship and express appreciation for the new spouse by accepting, loving, and providing support that will benefit the children and make the transition easier.

In the case of emotional, physical, and sexual abuse you must stand up to protect yourself, your children, and others who need an advocate. Pray fervently for God to guide you into truth. If you feel uncomfortable and unsafe about a situation that is happening with you or someone else, then do something. Faith requires action. Do not passively sit by and allow the abuse thinking it will go away. The abusive person will not change unless they understand that there will be a consequence for their crime.

Stand for righteousness making it very clear that abuse must never happen. State that if it does, the consequence will be that you will call the police, he will lose his family and home, and you will testify against him or her. When you say it, mean it. Be serious and get a plan in place. Is it work, is it uncomfortable, and is it scary? Yes, yes, yes, but God is with you. He says, *"Be strong and courageous. Do not be terrified. Do not be discouraged for I am with you wherever you go" (Joshua 1:9).* With God you have the power to protect yourself and others. The abusive person needs the transforming truth of God's Word and you just may be the vessel God will use to speak truth in love.

If you are a single woman, let me warn you as God does in His Word to be very careful who you allow into your home. When you are emotionally weak and hurt you become susceptible to men and women who can put on pretenses or appear spiritual, but are like wolves parading around in sheep's clothing to pressure you into a relationship. They manipulate their way into your home with deception as Tom did when my mother was vulnerable during her marriage struggles. Be alert and on guard. Listen to those family members and spiritual sisters and brothers in the church who love you and try to speak truth to you. Notice God's warning in the following verses:

> *People will be lovers of themselves, lovers of money, boastful...lovers of pleasure rather than lovers of God—having a form of godliness but denying its power. Have nothing to do with them. They are the kind who worm their way into homes and gain control over weak-willed women, who are loaded down with sins and are swayed by all kinds of evil desires, always learning but never able to acknowledge the truth (2 Timothy 3:2-8).*

This person may appear to be godly. Instead, he or she has selfish ambition for pleasure. They control people through pity, deception, a false sense of protection, and even can manipulate through prayer. Before you focus on any relationship seek God for wisdom and discernment. Choose to obey God, heal brokenness, change unhealthy behavior, and make every effort to protect your family. Otherwise, your children will make the same choices, even if they don't want to. They often will, because it's comfortable to follow in our parent's footsteps. With Jesus it's never too late to heal and change. Begin today. Eagerly anticipate what God will do as you seek Him with all of your heart to provide safety and protection.

Father God, you are my Protector and Provider. Your love always protects. Thank you for your powerful Word that protects me from going down the road of destruction. Thank you for sending Jesus to protect me from eternal separation from you. Thank you for the Holy Spirit that indwells in me as a temple of God to protect me from sinning against myself and others. Bought by the blood of Jesus, I want to honor you with my mind, body, and spirit. Thank you that at the beginning of creation you made us male and female to be united as husband and wife to become one flesh. Therefore what you have joined together, let no one separate, because you seek godly offspring. So guard me in my spirit, and keep me from breaking faith with my spouse, since you hate divorce and violence. Help me to establish goals in my difficult relationship to protect myself, my spouse, and the children in my life. Guard our hearts and minds in Christ Jesus. Lord, give me discernment of those who are lovers of themselves, lovers of money and pleasure rather than lovers of you, having a form of godliness but denying its power. Protect my family from those who worm their way into my life to gain control over my children or me. You are my hope and my salvation and I shall call on the name of the Lord to be safe. Help me to always learn, acknowledge, and obey your truth that will set me free to experience your peace and joy. In Jesus' name I pray. Amen.
1 Cor. 6:18-20, 13:7; Mark 10:6-9; Malachi 2:15-16; 2 Timothy 3:2-8.

GOD'S TRANSFORMING TRUTH
Establish the goal to protect to demonstrate love: "Love always protects." (1 Cor. 13:7)

QUESTION TO PONDER
What can you do to protect your difficult relationship?

TAKE ACTION
Decide how to protect the mind, body, and spirit of the person you struggle with as well as yourself.

Chapter Nine

STOP to Handle Anger

Everyone should be quick to listen, slow to speak and slow to become angry, for man's anger does not bring about the righteous life that God desires.
James 1:19-20

Jamie called me in a panic. "I need your help! I'm so angry I don't know what to do." He was having a problem with his unemployed roommate. She was behind on her rent, a bad influence on his children, as well as engaged in some business practices that caused the neighbors to complain. When Jamie talked to her she was unresponsive to his plea to take care of the problem and pay her back rent or move out. She then became angry, prompting Jamie to lash back. That's when she made unwarranted threats to call Child Protective Services. Jamie was furious. He adored his children and would do nothing to harm them. In fact, his fear of the possibility of losing custody due to false accusations caused him to call me for help.

Jamie needed some tools that he could implement right away. After I coached him, he called me the next day sounding like a different person. Joyfully he boasted that after he prayed God gave him self-control and the words to have a respectful and effective conversation with his roommate. He had peace and his fear subsided as he took the steps to get an attorney involved to protect himself and his children from the inappropriate behavior of his renter.

Anger is an emotion God gave us. We all have anger. It's your anger that prompts you to protect innocent people and fight for righteousness to bring about good. God desires for you to handle your anger appropriately. In fact, God says, *"In your anger do not sin" (Ephesians 4:26)*. Obviously, you can have anger without sinning. Otherwise, God would not have said so in His Word. Some people believe they don't have anger, since they don't lash out. The truth is that anger can manifest itself in critical thoughts, denial, withdrawal, depression, and forgetfulness. Quiet, non-responsive people can respond this way when emotionally or physically harmed. In fact, these people are just as angry. I know, because I was one of them.

What I told Jamie that day is that before you respond to someone who irritates, frustrates, or attacks you it's best to take a deep breath and STOP before you react. Let the following acrostic S.T.O.P. be your guide to gain self-control over your anger and perspective on the situation:

"S" is for SURRENDER to God to be lifted up: *"Submit yourselves to God. Resist the devil, and he will flee from you. Come near to God and he will come near to you...Humble yourself before the Lord and He will lift you up" (James 4:7-8, 10).*

"T" is for TRUST that God loves you and He will direct your path: *"Neither death nor life...nor anything else in all creation will be able to separate us from the love of God that is in Christ Jesus our Lord" (Romans 8:38-39). "Trust in the Lord with all your heart and lean not on your own understanding; in all your ways acknowledge Him, and He will make your paths straight" (Proverbs 3:5-6).*

"O" is for OBEY God to demonstrate love and see Him at work: *"Whoever has my commands and obeys them, he is the one who loves me. He who loves me will be loved by my Father, and I too will love him and show myself to him" (John 14:21).*

"P" is for PRAY to unleash God's power: *Jesus said, "If you remain in me and my words remain in you, ask whatever you wish, and it will be given you. This is to my Father's glory, that you bear much fruit, showing yourselves to be my disciples" (John 15:7-8).*

Let's look at Jesus as our example. Jesus always SURRENDERED to His Father's will, He TRUSTED that His Father loved Him, He OBEYED His Father, and He often PRAYED. Jesus demonstrated a righteous anger when religious leaders profited by taking advantage of His people. They had come to buy and sell their livestock to pay the temple tax and offer up their sacrifices. The scene plays out like this:

Jesus entered the temple area and drove out all who were buying and selling there. He overturned the tables of the money changers and the benches of those selling doves. 'It is written,' he said to them, 'My house will be called a house of prayer, but you are making it a 'den of robbers' (Matt. 21:12-13).

Jesus stood for righteousness and was motivated by unselfish desire to protect innocent people from unfair business practices. He rebuked the religious leaders for their greed and impure motives. He flipped over tables and told people to leave the temple. We should be motivated by the same goal to protect against those who bring physical, mental, emotional, or spiritual harm. In fact, God says that if we do not control our tongue, which can cause pain to others, or we fail to care for those who are suffering, then our religion is worthless. Let this scripture convict you to evaluate your priorities. Look at the following rebuke from James 1:26-27:

If anyone considers himself religious and yet does not keep a tight rein on his tongue, he deceives himself and his religion is worthless. Religion that God our Father accepts as pure and faultless is this: to look after orphans and widows in their distress and to keep oneself from being polluted by the world.

What breaks God's heart should break yours. You should fight against evil with a heart motivated by love. In the book, *Anger is a Choice*, Tim LaHaye and Bob Phillips make a distinct difference between God's anger and human anger. Man's anger is often uncontrolled without patience. Often men and women are motivated by hatred and resentment to seek revenge with the purpose to hurt

153

themselves or those who oppose them. Man's unrighteous anger breaks relationships. On the other hand, God's anger is controlled with purpose, never with hatred, malice, or resentment. God's anger is unselfish. It's an expression of concern to correct or curtail destructive behavior for the purpose to reconcile people to God.[10]

According to the biblical definition of love, we are not to become easily angered, nor are we to sin in our anger. This includes not being rude, selfish, or keeping a record of wrongs (Eph. 4:26; 1 Cor. 13:4-8). For when we do, our anger can turn to bitterness. A root of bitterness will cause us to lash out with venomous words; to withdraw or become defensive; to gossip, mock, joke, or become condescending; or to desire evil and revenge against a person.

STOP Before You React

Before you react, use the acrostic STOP (Surrender, Trust, Obey and Pray), and then implement the next four steps to ensure reconciliation. Otherwise, a root of bitterness can take hold, which leads to separation in your relationship with Christ and others.

1. **Listen and hold your tongue:** *"Everyone should be quick to listen, slow to speak and slow to become angry, for man's anger does not bring about the righteous life that God desires" (James 1:19-20).*
2. **Be self-controlled to demonstrate wisdom and gain respect:** *"A fool gives full vent to his anger, but a wise man keeps himself under control" (Proverbs 29:11).*
3. **Resolve anger quickly to avoid a root of bitterness:** *"In your anger do not sin: Do not let the sun go down while you are still angry, and do not give the devil a foothold" (Eph. 4:26-27).*
4. **Refuse to play the offense over and over in your mind:** *"Refrain from anger and turn from wrath; do not fret (or mull it over in your mind)—it leads only to evil" (Psalm 37:8).*

Anger is an emotion that God gave us control over by the power of the Holy Spirit that dwells within the believer. God would not tell us in James to be slow to anger if it were impossible to achieve success in this area. He warns us to listen before we say anything so not to become angry, knowing that anger does not promote a godly example (James 1:19-20). God yearns for us to be a reflection of His love that will bring others into a personal relationship with Christ. Whether we lash out in anger or pull away with condemning thoughts, unresolved anger is demeaning, disrespectful, and brings destruction to our relationships. Ultimately, uncontrolled anger destroys our testimony.

STOP to Determine the Blocked Goal

A blocked goal is often motivated by fear. When someone is angry, anxious or depressed, ask yourself *does this person think I am blocking them from their goal to feel protected, accepted, or successful?* If you determine that they believe you are blocking their goal, reassure him or her that your desire is to help them accomplish their goal and not to hinder it. It's important that they know with absolute assurance that you are for them and not against them. Communicate that you want to protect them from harm, encourage them to be all that God created them to be, accept them as a work in progress, and contribute to their well-being.

Instead of yelling to be heard or retaliating to punish or pulling away with unkind thoughts, identify the reason behind the anger. People have an innate desire to feel safe and accepted. God created us in His image with His divine nature to protect. God is our Protector. We know this to be true since Jesus died to protect you and me from eternal suffering. Not only that, He protects us in our daily comings and goings. Often we are completely oblivious of God's divine and supernatural protection.

The truth is that we have a loving Father who is the giver of every good and perfect gift. God's Word promises, *"If God is for us, who can be against us? He who did not spare his own Son, but gave Him up for us—how will He not also, along with Him, graciously give us all things?" (Romans 8:31-32)*. God in His grace and mercy has given us His Son to take the penalty of our sin, the Word of God to live by, and the Holy Spirit to comfort, counsel, and give us courage in all circumstances. Satan is the prince of this world until Jesus comes back to reign and rule. Until then, we will experience evil. Consider that God uses people like you and me to stand up to protect those who are being hurt, violated, and deceived by the enemy. As believers we have the power of God to protect people against evil. Ultimately, God uses His people to deliver a message of eternal healing to those who are hurting.

Ponder this idea, when we are unable to safeguard ourselves or others we fail to accomplish our inherent goal to protect. This inability to protect others and ourselves is contrary to the way God designed us. When we're unprotected at a young age we develop a coping mechanism. We live in denial or complacency and do nothing, we lash out in anger, or we runaway in hopelessness and despair. Often this is when we see someone turn to alcohol, drugs, cutting, starvation, violence, and sexual immorality as a means to escape the pain of the blocked goal to be protected. God created men and women to protect their children, but many become immobilized by a root of fear and bitterness when they themselves were abandoned, abused, or sexually used in childhood. Their state of helplessness, unable to take a stand to protect their own children, is often prompted by an inability to protect themselves as a child. This was the case with Patty's aunt in the previous chapter who was molested and allowed her husband to abuse her daughters and other girls. The cycle of abuse can continue for generations when we fail to protect our loved ones and ourselves.

God created the father to protect his family. In today's society many boys witness the physical or emotional abuse of their mothers. Feeling helpless, unable to standup to the abusive father figure, boys become defiant and bitter lashing out to harm others. In fact, our streets and prisons are full of hurt, helpless adult children who were unable to protect their mothers or felt threatened and unprotected themselves. Often hurt boys and girls seek ways to align themselves with those who will fight to protect them. They believe the twisted lie that they are loved by their gang. The truth is that often they are only accepted if they kill, steal, and fight the opposing gang to maintain the selfish agenda of the drug lords. The blocked goal to feel safe, accepted, and provided for will cause children and teens to fall prey to those who know how to manipulate and control with fear tactics. Imagine if these people knew the love of Jesus: His power, protection, and provision. Their lives would be transformed to live a life with purpose, knowing that God has plans to prosper them, and that they have a spiritual family who loves them. Let Kenji's story inspire you to have hope for those who are living in a prison of addiction, fear, pride, and unbelief.

Kenji's Testimony

Drugs, alcohol, and the wrong friends led Kenji down a path of destruction that he never imagined. Although Kenji was doing well in school and a star soccer player, he wanted to be accepted by his peers as he went into high school. Kenji joined a gang. He believed the lie that status, power, and recognition among his homies would bring purpose to his life and that these people cared about him. For sixteen years he proved his devotion to his gang members by destroying the opposing gang and protecting his own.

In and out of prison, Kenji failed to realize that his life of crime impacted not only his own life but also those who loved him most. Months went by where his parents and son went without hearing from him. Eventually, at a drug rehab program mandated by the state after his release from prison, Kenji met Charlene who managed the re-entry counselors working with parolees. When her supervisor position shifted to a new location, Kenji pursued her to discover the reason for her joy and passion for life. Learning of her love for Jesus, he invited Jesus into his heart as well.

Charlene never considered a relationship with someone previously incarcerated. She admits they made an unlikely pair, yet seeking God fervently she believed that God had brought Kenji into her life for a purpose. Establishing their relationship on God's principles they were married a few months later.

Over the years, Charlene had counseled and prayed with many family members devastated by the choices of the incarcerated, but she never fully understood their pain until two months into her own marriage. Kenji got drunk, which broke his parole and sent him back to prison for five more months. At that time, Charlene experienced firsthand the shame, guilt, and betrayal of her incarcerated husband. When she cried out to God on her knees, her heavenly Father comforted her with words of peace and purpose. She realized how that situation allowed her to comfort those who had loved ones in prison because she could now relate to their pain from their perspective. She trusted that God had a plan to use her and her incarcerated husband in ministry together. Charlene praised God and clung to His following promise:

Praise be to the God and Father of our Lord Jesus Christ, the Father of compassion and the God of all comfort, who comforts us in all our troubles, so that we can comfort those in any trouble with the comfort we ourselves have received from God (2 Cor. 1:3-4).

In prison, Kenji experienced true repentance and forgiveness before God when on his knees he completely surrendered his life to Jesus. Submitting himself to God, he grieved, mourned, and wailed for his double-mindedness. He came near to God and God came near to him. As Kenji humbled himself before God and resisted the devil by denouncing all his sin, Kenji was lifted up to discover true peace and joy for the first time (James 4:7-10). Immediately after his release, he publicly professed his faith in Christ through baptism. In a moment everything changed—delivered from his wrong thinking, his addictions, and his sixteen years as a gang member to live a life of purpose: to love and serve God.

Kenji was filled with a hunger and thirst to know God and follow Him. He realized that God protected him from knife wounds that missed major arteries and he dodged bullets that should have killed him. Instead of fighting on the streets, today Kenji and Charlene fight for families of inmates to stay hopeful and connected through the prison support group at their church. Together they testify to God's faithfulness and His transforming power.

STOP to Do the Battle

We must fight to protect our marriages, our children and grandchildren, and those who are hurting. First and foremost, do the battle on your knees in prayer. Pray for protection. Ask God to show you what you need to know. Your job is to determine what stronghold the enemy has on your loved one who is struggling. Stay vigilant and aware of what's going on. You may need to give up that glass of wine at night or going out with friends to come home on time to be on guard as to what is happening in your home. Listen to your gut. If you suspect misconduct, ask God to reveal truth.

If you suspect drug use with your teenagers then I suggest random drug and alcohol testing. Check-up on what your teen is doing, where they are, who they hang with, and talk to other parents to stay informed. I say this as I personally struggle to always know where my teenagers are, especially once they started driving. If you feel uncomfortable about a situation, don't allow inconvenience, apathy, or weariness to cause you to cave in to their demands. Our children need to hear the word *no*. Teens often test the boundaries or rules to see if their parents will do the battle to enforce the rules and consequences. They want to know that we care and we will fight for them!

Struggles are the tools that God allows to bring glory to Himself and hope to others. Through the process of loving challenging people, God loves you and prepares you for His mighty plan. God sets you free from the bondage of sin that causes destructive relationships. God's Word says, *"You, my brothers, were called to be free. But do not use your freedom to indulge the sinful nature; rather, serve one another in love" (Galatians 5:13)*. God wants you to trust Him in the difficult circumstance instead of turning to your sinful nature of pride, bitterness, fear, and unbelief.

Trust that God loves you and that He will guide you in the way you should go (Proverbs 3:5-6). Fortunately, Charlene did not give up on

159

her husband who backslid into his familiar ways. Jesus delivered Kenji of his destructive lifestyle as Charlene trusted God and accepted her husband as a work in progress. Daily they pray and read God's Word together. They have established guidelines that would protect their marriage and family. A wonderful retired Christian man came alongside Kenji to mentor him over the phone with biblical truth several times a week. Kenji meditated on God's Word and was set free from anger, destructive thinking, and wrong relationships. Now Kenji is a responsible member of society, a wonderful husband and father, and employed at his church.

Change takes time as you put God's principles into place. God is faithful to His promises, but you have to know them and follow them to claim them. Claim the following promise as your own:

Blessed is the man who does not walk in the counsel of the wicked or stand in the way of sinners or sit in the seat of mockers. But his delight is in the law of the Lord, and on his law he meditates day and night. He is like a tree planted by streams of water, which yields its fruit in season and whose leaf does not wither. Whatever he does prospers (Psalm 1:1-3).

Meditate on God's Word that it may penetrate your heart. Do not just listen to the Word or read it, but do it. You will know in your spirit what to do according to His Word. A few years ago, I cried out to God for my family to experience the promises that He had for us of peace, joy, and unity. In the book of Joshua chapter 6 we learn about how God tore down the walls of Jericho, a city filled with evil, when the Israelites' entered the Promised Land that was filled with His extravagant provisions described as milk and honey. At the time, the lies of the enemy were causing huge walls of division in my home. God desires for us to live in His Promised Land of abundant blessings as we follow Him. When I read this story in my spirit I knew I was to march around the outside walls of my house seven days in a row and pray. On the last day I walked around seven times as He instructed Joshua. This may sound crazy, but I had to be obedient to what I felt God wanted me to do. Otherwise, I might miss out on the blessings He had for my family.

I awoke early each morning beginning on Monday when my husband happened to be out of town for business. Raising my hands, I called out on the Lord to deliver my family from evil, to break down the walls of bitterness, unforgiveness, and anger. I prayed for the restoration and healing of my relationships with my husband and children. At first, I felt awkward as I feared my neighbors might see me at 6 in the morning with my hands raised high. But I decided it was more important to be obedient to what God told me to do than worry about what the neighbors might think of me.

On the seventh day I walked around my house seven times. Each time I went around I set a large stone by the gate as an altar to the Lord and as a reminder of how many times I went around. After my final lap, with hands held high, I bowed down on my knees at my back porch begging God for deliverance. As I finished praying I noticed an image through the window of my back door. There was my husband looking at me shaking his head. Once inside the house, Mark said, "That was weird."

Uncomfortable, I chuckled and replied, "Well, I don't think praying for my family is weird." He shrugged his shoulders and walked out of the room. A couple weeks later the walls of deception came down as we discovered that our daughter stole our car.

Kayla's Testimony

My daughter, Kayla, had just turned sixteen when she stole my car in the middle of the night to see her boyfriend. Before I realized she had stolen the car I had reported it stolen. When the police asked me what I wanted to do, I contemplated sending her to juvenile hall knowing she needed a severe consequence. Stealing a car was a felony. After careful consideration and a quick prayer for wisdom I made no official charges against her, but I was crushed in my spirit that she had broken our rules.

Furious at her boyfriend, at first I prohibited her from seeing him. Then I received some wise counsel from my sister Karen. As a teenager, prior to her running away, my mother had prohibited her from seeing a boy. My sister rebelled. If you remember from the first chapter, Karen was missing for four months when she finally came home pregnant. Tempted to project my sister onto my daughter, I made a conscious decision to determine that my daughter was not the same person as my sister and I fervently prayed against the generational sin of sexual immorality, teen pregnancy, and a rebellious spirit.

Learning from her own experience, Karen guided me to make arrangements to meet with my daughter and her boyfriend. My plan was to set up goals to protect them from a road of destruction by defining a healthy relationship. The boy never wanted to meet with us and the relationship ended. Although my daughter felt rejected she learned that he was not willing to respect her or her parents.

This situation prompted my husband and me to seek help. The walls of our hearts crumbled as we met with the pastor of our church. My prayer was answered as we began to get counseling from a Christian counselor that offered us wisdom. It was a step in the right direction. We gained insight that helped our relationship reach a new level at that time.

STOP to Discipline

Sometimes the greatest gift we can give is discipline. Other times, we show grace with a warning. Through prayer God will direct you. For stealing the car we put Kayla on restriction and gave her the consequence of not getting her driver's license until she was eighteen. With that consequence I drove her around town for the next two years. Nevertheless, she learned a valuable lesson that her choices impact other people, that there can be long-term ramifications, and a loss of privileges for wrong behavior. I communicated my love for my daughter by disciplining her as God disciplines us. He says,

> *My son, do not despise the Lord's discipline, and do not resent His rebuke, because the Lord disciplines those He loves, as a father the son he delights in (Proverbs 3:11-12).*

Loving discipline protects people from making the same bad choices in the future. We must communicate clearly that every choice we make will impact not only ourselves but others. Without a car it became evident to my daughter how her choices had consequences, not only to her but they impacted me. It was a valuable lesson that she learned, but not right away.

Remember that your children face tremendous pressures today. You have a short amount of time while they are impressionable. Fight for righteousness and truth. Do the battle for them by staying vigilant on your knees. The enemy lurks around like a roaring lion waiting to devour them and lure them away through the temptations and lies of this world (1 Peter 5:8). As parents we are to love them, pray for them, guide them, and discipline them or else they will be destroyed by their evil desires.

Sometimes it seems impossible to do it all. Many of us work all day and then come home to the demands of our children. But remember that we have resurrection power in Jesus. He will strengthen, guide, and empower you to discipline your children and those who are difficult to love. God gives you discernment when you stop to listen and wise-up to understand. When they act out in anger there's a reason and it's your job to figure out why. As you stay *joyful in hope, patient in affliction, and faithful in prayer (Romans 12:12)* God will show you what you need to know. I saw this happen with Kayla.

My heart broke as she engaged in sex, drugs, and alcohol. Three years after she stole my Suburban I felt extremely discouraged that none of my children loved God. Daily I cried out to Him. But on this one particular day I mourned, grieved, and wailed my double-mindedness. Kayla asked me to visit her at work that evening. Reluctantly, I followed through on my commitment by going out in the stormy weather. At the coffee shop where she worked, she shared with me what was happening in her life. Over the past couple of weeks she had read her Bible, prayed to God, and began tithing to our church. In awe of God's perfect timing to encourage my heart, I practically fell to my knees in that coffee shop as I praised God for His faithfulness.

If you struggle with a defiant teen, let Kayla's story be an inspiration to you. Instruct your children in the ways they should go, make the plan to protect with loving discipline, and use the acrostic STOP to avoid reacting with anger. Kayla now ministers to the hearts of teenage girls who are struggling to stand up against the pressures of this world in the high school and college setting. Through her own past struggles Kayla has a testimony that girls can relate to. God is using her immoral choices of the past to bring about good as she leads people to Christ.

STOP to Say What You Want

If you feel resentful and angry that some people take and take and take then this is a clue that you may have a problem. More than likely you have not communicated your expectations or goals effectively. In fact, you may have ideals of what you want in your head without ever verbalizing them. Often we can become angry when people fail us or imposition us, but we have allowed them to do it. When you explain calmly what you want, then you won't play victim or feel taken advantage of. At the same time, it's important to evaluate your motives. Why are you saying yes or no? Are you saying "yes" to something because you feel manipulated, controlled, fearful, or sorry for the person? People can manipulate and control you by trying to make you feel guilty or lashing out in anger. Allowing someone to control you is not healthy for you nor that person. Likewise, you need to respect others when they say "no" without making them feel guilty for their decision or trying to control them with your anger of lashing out, pulling away, or pouting.

Your reason to say "yes" or "no" should be for the purpose of protecting yourself or the other person. For instance, since I work from home it was easy for my teens to assume that I would drop everything to drive them to their destination. Often I felt used and disrespected with their demands, since they failed to see that I was working. Once I learned to clearly say what I wanted, my anger subsided. I could gently remind them of our agreement to plan ahead or to approach me with their request without the expectation that I would comply instantly.

Communicate your Desire to Protect

Our goal to protect should be communicated clearly to avoid unrealistic expectations that may prompt a root of bitterness, disapproval, and disappointment. Trust is built upon the understanding that we feel safe with that person. Make a conscience decision and agreement to protect your mind, body, and spirit. Not only protect yourself, but choose to protect the person you're in conflict with. If you can agree ahead of time, before an argument happens, use the words "safe" or "protect" as a reminder at the time of the argument. You can say, "I want you to feel safe." "I want to protect your heart." or "I don't feel safe right now."

Imagine the person's heart in the palm of your hand. God has given us a responsibility to protect the heart of our spouse, our children, and those in our realm of influence. When speaking to our children, or those in our custody, we must communicate that it's our job to protect them. Use the following words as a guide:

"It's my responsibility to protect you. I want to keep you safe. To do that, we must establish guidelines or rules to live by for your protection. I love you and I want you to know that I accept you, but I don't always agree with what you do. When you break the rules then there will be consequences."

Depending on the maturity level of who you're talking with, discuss the reason for your decision when conflict arises. The purpose is to alleviate their fear of being controlled or blocked from doing what they desire, which might be their driving force to be confrontational.

Communicate Your Contributions

For years I never understood what motivated my husband's anger. Finally, when Mark and I decided to establish the goal to protect one another and our family, we were surprised we wanted the same things. We had expectations that were never communicated. For instance,

Mark felt unsupported when he went away on business. When he called from out of town questioning me about homework I felt accused, defensive, and controlled. He believed that I would be uninvolved with our son's homework, because in the past I was distracted.

After we made the goal to protect, I understood his desire to protect our children. He didn't want them to fall behind in their homework or fail a test that might cause them to be ill-equipped for the next concept. I reassured my husband that we had the same goal to contribute to the academic growth of our children. With a concentrated effort I focused my attention on accomplishing the homework when my husband was out of town. My husband's anger was alleviated by my desire to come alongside him in the goal to help our kids to do well in school. Not only did Mark and I decide how to handle homework when my husband was out of town, but we determined how each of us would contribute daily according to our area of expertise. He was the go-to-man for math problems, where I helped with English assignments and art projects, and all concerns that came up in school. Other areas of contribution include:

- ➢ Time spent together
- ➢ Physical touch through hugs or physical intimacy in marriage
- ➢ Attitude of appreciation and affirmation
- ➢ Service through cooking, cleaning, shopping, home maintenance, and financial provision
- ➢ Caring, nurturing, and spiritual growth

Mark and I had decided when I lost my job at Nordstrom that I would stay home to raise our children. Mark provided financially and he had certain expectations of what I would be responsible for as a mother and wife. The problem was that we failed to communicate our expectations. My mother was my example. She worked full-time and kept busy with projects around the home. Early on, Mark was frustrated that my focus was on creating businesses, decorating, shopping, and then endless hours of writing. His expectation when the kids were young was that I would spend time on the floor reading and teaching them. For this reason, I felt inadequate as a mom, not always by what he said, but mostly through his facial expressions. I did the same thing to him. We needed to communicate what it meant for me to be a mom and wife, and for him to be a dad and husband. Even with our children we must communicate their contribution to the relationship. We must have team mentality to be successful. Communicate clearly what each will do to contribute and you will be amazed at the outcome.

Communicate Your Financial Goals

Some people are savers and others are spenders. An area of constant contention was when I spent money without asking about our finances. I blocked my husband's goal to be financially responsible. Once I aligned my priorities, I reassured him that we had the same goal of saving money. I demonstrated this through budgeting, open communication about purchases, and checking with him about finances before spending. We relieved stress by allotting a certain amount each week to spend on lunch or coffee or incidentals. Our weekly allowance, that we took out in cash, gave us freedom while we stayed within our budget. His anger was not about trying to control me, but trying to prevent us from going into debt. His motivation was to protect our family.

Communicate Your Personal Goals

It's important to communicate what you believe God has called you to do. Although your passion may be aligned with God's purpose, if your good intentions cause conflict in the home this may indicate a need to wait on God's perfect timing. A perfect example of this was when our children were young. I professed my desire to proclaim the gospel to the world. Mark's lack of enthusiasm confused me. I felt unsupported. In my mind, he blocked my goal. Fortunately his comment, "We have four small children. How do you expect to be an international speaker?" clued me into the fact that the timing was wrong for our family. Although I still judged him at the time, thinking that he was less of a Christian, since he did not share my desire to obey the Great Commission in the same way that I did.

Years later, I discovered Mark felt rejected, alone, and unsupported when I blocked our original goal for me to stay home to raise our children. Although I resented Mark at the time for blocking my goal, I needed the support of my husband to go into ministry. Fortunately, God used my husband to lead me. Over the years Mark has been supportive of my writing, evangelizing the neighborhood, and leading Bible studies. Looking back over the past sixteen years God had to work in my heart before I could ever publish this book or speak to the multitudes.

Holy Spirit, I praise you that you are with me. I need you to help me. Before I react please help me to remember to STOP. I SURRENDER and humble myself to you to be lifted up. I TRUST that you love me and I will not lean on my own understanding for you promise to guide my path. I OBEY you to demonstrate my love and see you at work. I PRAY to unleash your power as I remain in you and your words remain in me. This is to your glory, that I bear much fruit, showing myself to be your disciple. Let me be quick to listen, slow to speak and slow to become angry, to live the righteous life that you desire. Help me be self-controlled to demonstrate wisdom and gain respect. Help me to not let the sun go down while I am still angry to avoid giving the devil a foothold. Help me to not play the offense over and over in my mind for it leads only to evil. Show me the blocked goals that are causing conflict with _____. In Jesus' name I pray. Amen.
James 4:10; Romans 8:38-39; Proverbs 3:5-6; John 14:21; John 15:7-8; James 1:19-20; Proverbs 29:11; Ephesians 4:26-27; Psalm 37:8.

GOD'S TRANSFORMING TRUTH
STOP to handle anger to become righteous: "Everyone should be quick to listen, slow to speak and slow to become angry, for man's anger does not bring about the righteous life that God desires." (James 1:19-20)

QUESTION TO PONDER
What are some of the blocked goals that are causing conflict?

TAKE ACTION
STOP to identify what you want for the relationship and establish an action plan on how to achieve your goal to protect.

Chapter Ten

Take Responsibility

*Confess your sins to each other and
pray for each other so that you may be healed. The
prayer of a righteous man is powerful and effective.*
James 5:16

We fell asleep angry. When I woke up, it was still dark. Snow covered the ground in Whistler, British Columbia. It was Good Friday, but nothing felt good about it at 3 a.m. Feeling the distance that separated me from my husband who lay next to me, I stared at the ceiling and shouted silently from underneath the blankets, *"Why God? Why can't my marriage be the way I want?"*

Really, I knew there was no such thing as a perfect marriage, but I was frustrated that over the years we fell back into the same patterns of dysfunctional behavior. Then I heard God's still small voice, not audible but in my head, *"For the sake of the ministry endure the hardships."* He had given me this message ten years before when I wanted to leave my marriage. Back then God asked, *"Are you willing to wait ten years for the marriage you desire?"* I had said yes, but now I cried out to God, *When will he change?*

In that moment, God reminded me of how my marriage had improved over the years. Was it perfect? No. But my husband and I were celebrating our twenty-fifth anniversary. We had held the family together and we had built some nice memories. I sighed, knowing God was trying to talk to me, but I still wasn't ready to listen. I dozed back to sleep.

In the morning I grabbed my ski jacket to head out the door for some breakfast items before packing the SUV to leave Whistler behind. Arriving at the local market I discovered that the store was closed for another thirty minutes. In seconds I spotted a coffee shop. Running in from the snow, I found a table where I warmed up with my hot latte. I pulled out my pocket Bible buried in my purse and opened randomly to a page. I began to read from 2 Corinthians 5:18-20.

All this is from God, who reconciled us to himself through Christ and gave us the ministry of reconciliation: that God was reconciling the world to himself in Christ, not counting men's sins against them. And he has committed to us the message of reconciliation. We are therefore Christ's ambassadors, as though God were making his appeal through us.

My eyes began to water. I felt God's presence in the crowded coffee shop. God, in His great mercy, lovingly reminded me to be reconciled to my husband. Christ had humbled himself to die a brutal death on my behalf, now I was being asked to die to myself, to have a spirit of reconciliation and kindness towards my husband. I looked down to continue reading.

We put no stumbling block in anyone's path, so that our ministry will not be discredited. Rather, as servants of God we commend ourselves in every way: in great endurance; in troubles, hardships and distresses (2 Cor. 6:3-5).

Again, God was talking to me. The same scripture that I thought about in the dim hours of the morning were to endure the hardships for the sake of my ministry. I sighed knowing God was giving me a message. Pride had kept me from apologizing to my husband. Frustrated that I was the one who always had to apologize first, God was convicting me. Although I had asked Mark earlier, in front of the children, if something was wrong he had said no. But I knew he was mad. Instead of confronting him again, I had pulled away and put up a wall. My mind had gone to unkind thoughts.

In that busy coffee shop, before God, I confessed my sin of bitterness, resentment, and pride. When I returned to the condo, I reached out to my husband with a hug knowing he felt loved when I did. I humbly asked for his forgiveness for pulling away. With my confession Mark then opened up about how I had hurt him by a critical remark I made to our friends earlier in the week. I took responsibility for my critical spirit, realizing that I had held onto bitterness from an earlier episode where he lashed out at me. We had discussed the situation, but there was still residue. This time we embraced and apologized.

Celebrating Easter a couple of days later, I realized that Jesus surrendered to death on a cross. He humbled himself to later ascend to heaven with resurrection power. When we humble ourselves to say, "I'm sorry," the same resurrection power is available to us. With humility God promises that He will heal us and He will give us powerful and effective prayers.

Confess your sins to each other and pray for each other so that you may be healed. The prayer of a righteous man is powerful and effective (James 5:16).

Take responsibility for your sin so you may experience God's grace and power. Certainly, we can be unlovable. We allow pride to rear its ugly head of defensiveness and unkind thoughts. When I check my motives and humble myself before God and the person I'm upset with, then I find mercy and reconciliation. After years of resenting my husband for his intense, no nonsense, analytical approach to our conversations, I now try to step back for a moment to understand where he's coming from. I try to remember to STOP to listen, to acknowledge what he says, and not argue.

Responsible for your Heart

Ask yourself, what is God trying to tell me through this person? More than likely, you are part of the problem. Sometimes your contribution to the conflict can be so subtle and deceptive. You can feel justified for your selfish motives, ungrateful attitude, critical thoughts, and the cruel words that are a reflection of your heart, taught in the chapter *Motivated by a Pure Heart*. The obvious is your sinful actions, but we must not brush aside the possibility of the internal sin of casting judgment.

When you have a heart of condemnation, God may test your heart by allowing the conflict. In Luke 6:37 Jesus warns, *"Do not judge and you will not be judged. Do not condemn, and you will not be condemned. Forgive, and you will be forgiven."* Judgment is looking down on someone and thinking you could never be that way, thinking that you are better. We are all capable of bad behavior. All sin is wrong in the sight of God and separates us from Him and people. We must examine our motives, attitudes, and thoughts to get to the root of our critical judgments. When we approach a situation with empathy not criticism, we are less likely to judge.

Steve's Testimony

Sometimes we think people are unlovable by the way they look and their lifestyle. This happened to me. God used a tall scrubby bearded man with filthy clothes and worn out shoes. This homeless man plopped down on the leather chair at a local coffee shop. Separated only by a small table and a different life experience, I recognized this God encounter.

Nervous to talk to him, God nudged me to ask, "Can I buy you a cup of coffee?" The gruff man lifted his head when he heard my voice. His tender eyes met mine and he nodded with enthusiasm, "Sure. I would like that."

When I returned with the coffee and pastry he politely thanked me for the kind gesture. Delighted to make his day and surprised by his gentleness I asked, "So what brings you to this community?"

That's when I heard Steve's story.

Sitting next to him, he spoke coherently of his past and was aware of his pride that prevented him from getting help.

I proclaimed, "God has a plan and a purpose for your life. It's a miracle you're even alive. God has protected you."

Straightening up in his chair Steve looked encouraged. The weathered face of this forty-nine year old man grinned under his large crooked nose and said, "You have *no idea* what God has saved me from," nodding as he reminisced in his thoughts, "I'm very thankful."

Talking to this man convicted me. We had taken two different paths, but God brought us together in a coffee shop for a purpose.

Before I left, I offered to pray for Steve and he welcomed my prayer for protection, wisdom, and courage to get the help he needed. I recognized how his countenance had changed from when I first met him. Delighted when Steve promised to go to the Rescue Mission, I gave him a hug. Filled with joy that God could use me, I hoped he would take the steps in the right direction to make a new normal. As I walked away I realized this wasn't about God using me, but God using a homeless man to show me how much I had to be grateful for. A warm cup of coffee, a roof over my head, food in the cupboard, and my convenient lifestyle I had taken for granted. I became grateful for a homeless man who gave me a new perspective.

When you judge, keep in mind that you could have gone down the same path of unrighteousness with a different set of circumstances. When you find you have a critical spirit toward someone who is overweight, in prison, homeless, addicted to drugs or alcohol, uneducated, unbelieving, lashing out in anger, engaged in sexual immorality, or acting unlovable, immediately STOP. Don't jump to conclusions and accusations. First, put yourself in their shoes. It is by the grace of God that you are not in their situation. Instead of judgment, show compassion. Ask God for wisdom as you ponder their past pain, their perspective, and their personality taught in the chapter *Wise-Up to Understand*.

Ask the Holy Spirit to reveal truth. If you remember that God is allowing conflict for a purpose then it can change your perspective. Maybe God wants to reveal Himself to you through your obedience to do the right thing. He may want to give you a new revelation of Himself. Ask God to show you what He's doing in the situation and where you're at fault. Pride causes us to blame and accuse the other person by thinking we're better than they are, which prevents resolution from taking place. God says in Matthew 7:5, *"First take the plank out of your own eye, and then you will see clearly to remove the speck from your brother's eye."*

Often, you are to blame for a portion of the problem due to your attitude and your response. Although the other person could have started the conflict try not to determine who contributed more. Take responsibility for your actions and attitude, humble yourself, agree to what you did to contribute, and apologize. The words, "I'm sorry I hurt your feelings" or "You're right I didn't listen" are powerful tools to acknowledge that you are in agreement with an area of what they are communicating. Just make sure when you say these words that you mean them, otherwise you are being deceitful, which is wrong and God calls it evil (Matt. 5:37).

Responsible for Denial and Exaggerations

Denial is when you are unwilling to receive or accept a negative comment. Instead of looking at your own behavior you attack and accuse others. You may redirect the conversation back to the other person's faults or past, blaming them for the entire conflict. If you are in a state of denial you may be blind to your own behavior or what is going on in your relationship. Sometimes it's your way to cope at the time with unbearable circumstances.

Examples of Denial:
➤ Deflecting the blame back onto the other person.
➤ Redirecting the conversation to that person's past/current wrongs.
➤ Using guilt-trips or self-pity as a way to "get out of it."
➤ Chalking the problem up to his/her "inaccurate perception."

Exaggerations are the way people accuse others by making comments that define a person. The enemy will use people to do his dirty work. Look at the person who is attacking you or falsely accusing you as having a stronghold from the enemy. Do not be defensive, but be open to hear constructive criticism. Ask God what He is trying to tell you. Be careful not to use generalizations like the following:

Examples of Exaggeration:
➢ "I can't believe he did that; what a selfish person."
➢ "Only a heartless woman would say such a thing."
➢ "You always _____." or "You never _____."

Denial and exaggerations are unhealthy ways that avoid taking responsibility for your actions. Usually someone on the outside can see more clearly what is happening in the relationship. Often it's a good idea to have someone give you their honest input. A Christian counselor, faith coach, or pastor can give clarity as an uninvolved third party. Ask them to be honest with you so you can change to be all that God wants you to be. Welcome constructive criticism as God can use other members of the church body to impart wisdom and correction. Be self-reflective. Always search yourself for how you may have contributed to the conflict.

Responsible for Triangulation

A triangle can occur when two people are interacting and a third party pipes in to voice their opinion, to defend or side with one of the two parties. I was a pro at this. There were times after a long day at work that Mark came home tired and short tempered, raising his voice in frustration when the kids had failed to start their homework. For years I condemned him by intruding in the conversation in an attempt to side with my kids and rebuke my husband for his anger. Often I turned away and rolled my eyes in frustration, or gave another clue that I was upset, annoyed, and disappointed with his behavior. Finally, I realized that we were in a pattern that needed to change. My condemnation and interference never helped the situation, but hindered the relationship. His relationship was between each of them, not about me as a third party. We were caught in a family triangle.[11]

Let me clarify, that as we learned earlier, we should do everything to protect our children if they are being abused. In a non-abusive situation we have no business getting involved. I often stepped into the middle of a conversation by defending, justifying, and making comments that interfered and caused conflict. My children did the same thing with their siblings. My husband is responsible for his relationship with each of his children independent of me. I don't have to try to control that relationship by interfering, making suggestions, or talking behind his back. I'm just as responsible in my relationships with family and friends.

When I explained to my husband that I was no longer participating in conflicts by saying comments or thinking negative thoughts, but instead letting him work out his own relationships, my husband responded with gratefulness. I clarified with my husband that if there was any form of physical abuse or I felt they were being emotionally beat down that as their mother it was my responsibility to protect my children. I made it clear that I would not hesitate to call the police in the case of violence. My husband agreed that calling the police would be the right thing to do.

Be aware of triangles in your relationships. Triangles happen anytime a third person becomes involved in a relationship. Gossip and slander are another example of a triangle. Instead of going to the individual whom the problem is with, the person complains to a third party. Complaining opens the door for destruction. I advocate doing life together but not as a gripe session. God designed the church to be there for your sisters and brothers, but you must have the right motives when you seek godly counsel. Sharing your frustration with someone should be for the purpose of gaining proper perspective as well as to gain the tools that will equip you to speak the truth in love to the difficult person. Most importantly, establish accountability with those whom you seek godly counsel. If someone complains about a third party the best way to avoid the pitfall of triangulation is to stop to think about how to provide wise counsel so not to contribute to the destruction of that relationship. With humility and kindness, encourage reconciliation by teaching God's transforming truths. Tell them about confessing their sin to one another to be healed or to pray for wisdom from God who will give generously. You might consider sharing the STOP acrostic or how to speak truth in love that will bring maturity and growth taught in the next chapter. This final truth is important to communicate to the person who is sharing with you. Otherwise, they may avoid an important conversation that could resolve the conflict.

Responsible for Avoidance

By avoiding the difficult conversation you allow the inappropriate behavior to continue. Indirectly, you imply that the behavior is allowed. It's important to understand that you are part of the conflict if you are allowing sinful behavior to continue. Recognize your responsibility to seek reconciliation. When you fail to follow what God directs you to do, it is considered sin. In Matthew 18:15-17 it is written,

> *If your brother sins against you go and show him his fault, just between the two of you. If he listens to you, you have won your brother over. But if he will not listen, take one or two others along, so that every matter may be established by the testimony of two or three witnesses.*

In other words, after you attempt to talk to the person about his sin several times and he still has an unrepentant heart then get help from a third party. A counselor can offer a new perspective. To convince your brother or sister to repent you must speak truth in love with humility, a gentle spirit, and covered in prayer for the purpose to reconcile him to God. This will be discussed in the next chapter. Learn from Jacob how important it is to seek reconciliation and how to do it with humility.

Jacob's Testimony

In Genesis 25 - 33, there's a story of twin brothers, Esau and Jacob, who fought from the time they were in their mother's womb. Esau was favored by his father Isaac, and Jacob by his mother Rebekah. When Isaac was nearly blind and ready to pass away from old age, he planned to bless his oldest son Esau. Yet Rebekah deceived her husband to give the blessing to her favored son Jacob. Esau was filled with anger and rage when he discovered the deception of his younger brother who took his birthright and stole his blessing. When Jacob discovered his brother's intention to kill him, he fled four hundred miles to the north to Haran where his uncle Laban lived.

Twenty years had passed since Jacob had last seen his brother Esau. Jacob prepared to reconcile with his brother by having a humble heart, seeking God until He would bless him, and sending gifts of livestock ahead with a message that elevated his brother to lord and referred to himself as his brother's servant. Jacob approached Esau in the distance by bowing down to the ground seven times. Esau embraced his brother and they both wept and kissed. Jacob's humility brought healing to the relationship. God promises in the following scripture that He will lift you up when you humble yourself:

> *All of you clothe yourselves with humility toward one another, because, 'God opposes the proud but gives grace to the humble.' Humble yourselves, therefore, under God's mighty hand, that He may lift you up in due time (1 Peter 5:5-6).*

Jacob demonstrated humility, repentance, and responsibility by his actions of bowing down and calling his brother lord and through the words he said recorded in Genesis 33:10 to his brother, *"If I have found favor in your eyes, accept this gift from me. For to see your face is like seeing the face of God, now that you have received me favorably."* God blessed Jacob's humble heart with reconciliation.

Responsible for being Unapproachable

You become unapproachable when you are seen as unsafe to talk to. You contribute to the conflict by being uninterested, unpredictable, short-tempered, judgmental, punitive, hypersensitive, argumentative, or unfriendly. People will be less likely to raise issues with you and the issues will remain unresolved if you are unapproachable and difficult.

It's imperative to be open to hearing what people have to say about a situation or a conflict involving you.

Instead of reacting, stop to listen. Ask God to show you the truth. Sometimes unhealthy behavior can feel comfortable. Withdraw, denial, overreacting, smothering are all symptoms of how people may be raised or taught to deal with various situations in childhood. Emotional connectedness is learned by those encounters we witness as children growing up or what has worked in the past. In an unhealthy environment behavior requires people to fight or act out to receive love. Despite the problems that come from the poor behavior it feels comfortable and natural. This pattern of dysfunction may continue to the next generation if you neglect to change the cycle. Each time you lash out or withdrawal you become unsafe to approach. Confess that sin to be healed of your unhealthy behavior.

Responsible for Defensiveness

There's no reason to be defensive. God may be trying to use the person to show you a sin or behavior that dishonors Him. Even if the person who is accusing you is judgmental, punitive, and harsh. STOP to listen to what they say instead of defending yourself. Ask God to show you what you did to contribute to the conflict. God wants to use you to demonstrate proper behavior by maintaining self-control, a humble and gentle spirit, and a contrite heart. You may need to confess to hurting someone's feelings, even when it was unintentional.
I finally did.

Kylie's Story
A wall of bitterness divided my eighteen-year-old daughter and me. We were complete opposites. Kylie was analytical; I was expressive. She was organized and a planner. I flew by the seat of my pants. Kylie was self-sufficient and self-motivated. In fact, I never had to worry about her doing homework or accomplishing the tasks that needed to be done. I appreciated that she was responsible and hard-working, but I never said it.

When Kylie made the comment to me that she had raised herself since the age of seven, when her brother had leukemia, I went on the defensive.

"What do you mean? Who drove you to your doctor appointments? Who chose to put you in the gifted program and drove you across town? Who took you to your sports after school and bought your clothes and cooked for you?"

I knew I did a good job of pointing out all the things I did over the past years, thinking I put her in her place. The problem was that my justification did not make the wall of bitterness come down. It only strengthened it. She wouldn't talk to me, she wouldn't eat my cooking, and when I attempted to hug her, well, it was like hugging a cold fish.

I began to seek God with all my heart to have Him restore my relationship with my daughter. I prayed fervently for wisdom. I raised my arms over the doorposts of her room like the Israelites did for protection over their children. I knelt like Jesus demonstrated when He cried out to His Father. I wept and prayed. My heart was broken. I wanted to be close to my daughter, but I didn't know how. Then God showed me. Kylie had tried to tell me, but I didn't listen.

I was the problem. I was defensive and unapproachable. I had rejected her by not spending time with her. I thought back to specific instances when she wanted me to put her to bed, or take the dog for a walk, or later when she was older, workout together—but I was too busy.

I asked Kylie out to lunch. She put me off, probably thinking I would preach to her. I insisted that she have lunch with me. I pursued her and didn't give up. She finally agreed to go. As we sat across the table from each other I asked her to forgive me for not being there for her. I explained that when she had tried to tell me before I had made excuses and justified my behavior. My eyes filled with tears, however I desperately tried to maintain my composure. I told her I wouldn't cry, since I knew she felt uncomfortable when I did. She smiled nervously and said, "Oh good," looking over at the waitress who was heading our direction.

No excuses came with my apology, no justification, no pointing out what I *did* do. Only heartfelt repentance brought down Kylie's wall of protection. She had guarded her heart against her mother's rejection for years. Finally, God showed me my pride. My wall of self-righteousness and defensiveness came down as I listened to my daughter's heart and took responsibility.

God wants to heal you and make you a new creation. He wants to restore your relationships. It happens with a repentant heart. God is faithful to hear the cry of your heart and cleanse you of all unrighteousness *"if you confess your sins He is faithful and just to forgive you and purify you of all unrighteousness" (1 John 1:9)*. Healing does not always come immediately, but eventually God will bring reconciliation when you start taking responsibility instead of demanding your rights.

In his powerful book, *Victory over the Darkness*, Dr. Neil Anderson shares valuable wisdom into our rights verses our responsibilities, which I have paraphrased as well as included my own interpretation. Ponder the concept that in marriage a husband does not have the right to have a submissive wife, but it's his responsibility to be a loving husband who dies to his own needs like Christ died for the church. Headship is not a right to be demanded, but an awesome responsibility to be fulfilled. Wives do not have the right to demand a spiritual husband, but it is her responsibility to be a submissive, supportive wife. Often when a woman has a spirit of humility her husband is more likely to step-up to be the spiritual leader because he's less threatened. Parents do not have the right to demand obedience, but it is their responsibility for disciplining, raising, and training their children in the Lord. In the church, as the body of Christ, we have the privilege and responsibility to love God with all our heart and to love others. Someday when we stand before a holy God we will be rewarded for how well we satisfied our responsibility.[12]

In some ways, maintaining relationships is a lot like walking the dog. We have to pick up the poop along the way. Otherwise, the sidewalk piles up with stinky stuff that others will step in. Irresponsible people leave their messes behind. In much the same way, when we avoid taking responsibility in our relationship we leave behind a pile of hurt feelings. Rejection, disapproval through facial expressions, put-downs, selfish motives, condescending remarks, and an attitude that says *I'm better than you* can cause people to feel insecure and bitter.

Our responsibility as Christians is to represent Jesus Christ through our ability to humble ourselves. We are set apart from this world through a repentant and humble heart. Our desire should be to reconcile differences as quickly as possible. God says to reconcile with those who have something against us (Matthew 5:23-24). Only then will people know us by our love. In the next chapter learn how to have that difficult conversation to bring healing.

Righteous Father, I praise you for your mercy and grace. I humble myself before you to confess my sin of (<u>bitterness, pride, slander, gossip, anger, and avoidance</u>). Thank you that when I confess my sins you are faithful and just to forgive me and purify me of all unrighteousness. With my confession, my prayers are powerful and effective. Empower me to not judge or condemn, so not to be judged or condemned by you, but to forgive _____ that I might be forgiven. Let me be sensitive to my sin that I do not gossip, but instead go and show _____ their fault, just between the two of us. If _____ refuses to listen may we find others to help us in our conflict to be a witness for your glory and praise when we are reconciled. Thank you for your promise that says when I humble myself, you will lift me up in due time. In Jesus' name I pray. Amen.
1 John 1:9; James 5:16; Luke 6:37; Matthew 7:5; 1Peter 5:5-6.

GOD'S TRANSFORMING TRUTH
Take responsibility in order to be healed: "Confess your sins to each other and pray for each other so that you may be healed" (James 5:16).

QUESTION TO PONDER
What sin are you justifying because of someone's behavior or attitude?

TAKE ACTION
Humble yourself by apologizing for your contribution to the conflict.

Chapter Eleven

Express Truth in Love

*Speaking the truth in love, we will in all things grow up
into Him who is the Head, that is, Christ.*
Ephesians 4:15

Hiding from conflict is never a good option. I learned this the hard way. Instead of expressing my feelings, I often avoided the situation and put on the mask of deception. Dishonest and clothed with self-righteousness, I prevented change and growth from taking place. I chose to bury the hurt, put up a wall of protection, and ignore the problems that would ultimately bring destruction. Deceived in my thinking, I thought it was easier to say nothing, unaware that my silence had separated me from people over the years. But worse, it separated me from God. He clearly says we must do everything possible to live in peace and reconcile our relationships so our worship can be pure:

> *Therefore, if you are offering your gift at the altar and there remember that your brother has something against you leave your gift there in front of the altar. First go and be reconciled to your brother; then come and offer your gift (Matthew 5:23-24).*

When we procrastinate and do not do what we know we should do we are sinning (James 4:17). This applies to reconciling a relationship and speaking truth to those we are in conflict with. Often we know what we should do, but we don't do it. Instead, angst and guilt keep us distant. Fear or pride can hold us captive with a root of bitterness until we step out in faith to trust God to guide us to reconciliation. Through our obedience to courageously confront a situation and speak the truth in love, we mature to become more Christ-like (Ephesians 4:15).

God wanted me to mature.

In the first chapter of this book, *Come out of Hiding,* I mentioned my best friend, neighbor, and spiritual mentor who I walked with five days a week. Pamela became an instrument in healing my past and developing my relationship with Jesus. She encouraged me relentlessly to attend her Bible study and often prayed for me. I confided in her about everything. In some ways, *she* became my rock and my security instead of Jesus.

As it turned out, my world crashed down on me when Connor became sick with leukemia. Pamela was not available as much as I needed her. I expected her to be by my side, yet we rarely saw one another. I became resentful and angry, ignoring some of her phone calls, because I was hurt. Occasionally when we did talk, I pretended everything was fine by becoming aloof.

Months after Connor's treatment, I arranged to meet with Pamela to talk about our relationship. Honestly, it was one of the hardest and bravest things I ever did. Although afraid of more rejection, I could no longer tolerate the torment of disconnectedness. Being honest, I told her how much I missed her and how I valued our friendship. Without condemnation, gently I sought understanding about her distance during Connor's illness. That's when she shared her heart with me.

Emotionally distraught, as Connor's Godmother, Pamela could hardly stomach the sight of my precious bald-headed son hooked-up to tubes in the hospital. Furthermore, during Connor's treatment Pamela had her own problems to deal with. She was busy caring for her elderly mother who was ill and living out of town. On top of that, she had dealt with an investigation against someone who had been stalking her.

With more understanding of what Pamela had experienced during that time, I felt horrible for pulling away. I extended compassion and took responsibility for my inappropriate behavior. Lovingly, I shared my feelings of rejection and she apologized that she wasn't there for me. We embraced and reconciled. By speaking truth in love our friendship was healed and we gained a deeper level of respect and appreciation for one another.

Often we have unrealistic expectations of people. God revealed that I had put Pamela on a pedestal with idealistic hopes that she would always be available to comfort me in my times of trouble. She became an idol as I expected her to meet my needs as well as be perfect. God used the pain of that situation to teach me to put my focus on Him. God is the only One who is perfect, He knows all of your needs, and He will always be there to comfort you.

Before I move on, it's important to let you know that this chapter will guide you to have a conversation with a person who is not prone to physical abuse and violence. My goal is to protect you. If you are in a physically abusive relationship seek professional help. Remember the greatest gift of love can be tough love. Sometimes, for safety reasons, the consequence may be a boundary that says, *I love you, but you have lost the privilege to be with me until you change your abusive behavior. God tells me that love always protects and I need to protect myself.* Appropriate discipline must be enforced to protect you and others against physical abuse as taught in the chapter *Establish the Goal to Protect*. A trained Christian counselor can help you through that process. At the same time, remember to call on the name of Jesus and fervently seek Him in prayer with others.

Certainly there are Christians who remain as spiritual babies in their walk with God. As a toddler is immature, demanding his own way with tantrums, a grown man or woman can act like a selfish untrained child. They act out in aggression or they run away from conflict. Often this inappropriate behavior continues because no one has stepped out in faith and obedience to confront the person in love regarding the issue. With humility and honesty, we speak truth boldly in love to be set apart for God's glory. We promote Christian maturity and build up the body of Christ as illustrated in the following scriptures:

Instead, speaking the truth in love, we will in all things grow up into him who is the Head, that is, Christ...Therefore each of you must put off falsehood and speak truthfully to his neighbor, for we are all members of one body (Ephesians 4:15, 25).

You must stop pretending that everything is okay when it's not. Every time you speak truth and trust God to handle the situation, you will mature. If God says in His Commandments that you shall not bear false witness against your neighbor, then you are not to lie (Exodus 20:16). Although it may appear easier to say nothing to avoid confrontation, it is essentially lying and deceitful. That sin will bring division to your relationship and separation from God. Jesus said in Matthew 5:37, *"Simply let your 'Yes' be 'Yes,' and your 'No,' 'No'; anything beyond this comes from the evil one."* This scripture is about being honest about what you want. Satan wants you to live in fear of what others will think, say, or do. Remember, *"God did not give us a spirit of fear, but a spirit of power, love, and sound mind" (2 Timothy 1:7)*. Through the spirit of God you are equipped to speak in love to difficult people. In fact, you must speak truth or you are no good to anyone. God says,

> *You are the salt of the earth. But if the salt loses its saltiness, how can it be made salty again? It is no longer good for anything, except to be thrown out and trampled underfoot (Matthew 5:13).*

You are called to be the salt of the earth by expressing truth with wisdom, grace, and gentleness (Colossians 4:5-7). God's truth can hurt. Imagine how salt in a wound can sting, yet it cleanses the wound to avoid infection. Salt was known as a preservative and for curing of meat before refrigeration. Not only can salt sting, but it can be tasty and appetizing if used sparingly. The truth of God is the same way. When you stand for righteousness be gentle, confident, and self-controlled to penetrate the heart, and cleanse and preserve the soul from the infection of destructive thinking and actions that lead to death.

With Christ you are a new creation. You are motivated by unselfish ambition and humility with an attitude of gratitude and praise for what God is doing and going to do. Your thoughts are focused on what is right, true, and praiseworthy to communicate with a pure heart. Ask yourself,

> ➤ What is my motivation behind speaking to this person?
> ➤ Do I want the best for this person or am I only interested in what's comfortable for me?
> ➤ Do I think I'm better?
> ➤ What am I grateful for that I can communicate?
> ➤ Do I have intentions to bring good, not harm?
> ➤ Am I promoting reconciliation to Christ and glorifying God by what I say?

Covered in prayer, remember to show confidence in God and respect for yourself. For all levels of conflict, be courageous to speak truth knowing God is with you. Whether addressing a spouse who is having an adulterous relationship or a teen addicted to drugs, be firm and self-controlled. In Dr. James Dobson's excellent book, *Love Must be Tough*, he teaches in the case of infidelity the importance to communicate confidence without whimpering or begging, but that you believe in yourself and that you portray that you will be alright whatever happens, whether they chose to stay or leave. The message clearly communicated is that if you won't honor me by being loyal and committed to me then leave. [13]

Your confidence is not about pride or revenge. In every difficult conversation it's about trusting that God's got your back and He wants to protect you and bring His people to repentance. Pray that God would go before you to prepare the heart of the person. Consider that prior to the conversation you should make an appointment to avoid interruption. Some people are planners, not spontaneous. Be prepared. Go through the following guide and write down the items in the parenthesis that apply to your relationship. Prior to sitting down with the person, you may need to practice the conversation with a friend. If it feels impossible to have a face-to-face dialogue (which nothing is impossible with God) then use this chapter as a guide for writing a letter without blaming or attacking. If you do decide to write a letter, you can choose to send it, but consider reading the letter aloud as I did with my Great Aunt Daisy and my mother. This opened the door for further discussion and understanding.

When you sit down to talk, before you begin, ask if you can invite God into the conversation. Have no expectations and do not condemn the individual if they do not feel comfortable with prayer. In fact, the person may feel unsafe to pray with you due to past circumstances and fear of condemnation. In most cases, consider your conversation to be the first of many. To guide your discussion with the difficult person consider using the simple acrostic A.C.T.S.:

"A" stands for Affirm your Love and Appreciation
"C" stands for Confess Sins to Take Responsibility
"T" stands for Tell the Truth with Thanksgiving
"S" stands for Say what you want with a Solution

Early on in my Christian walk this acrostic was taught to me in a similar way to guide my conversation with God. In the same way, it's just as effective to guide our conversations with people.

Affirm your Love and Appreciation

Before you get started, consider that physical touch is a powerful way to communicate connection and that you care. When appropriate, hold or touch their hand or arm as you begin to communicate with sincerity. Sometimes they will pull away and that's alright.

Affirm your love, even if you do not feel the emotion of love. Remember love is an action: patient, kind, humble, gentle, unselfish, forgiving, truthful, protective, trusting, hopeful, persevering, and faithful (1 Cor. 13:4-7). When you begin the conversation emphasize that you want the best for the person. Express your love, deep concern, and care for their well-being.

Follow God's instructions to speak what is helpful for building others up to benefit him or her (Ephesians 4:29). The person needs to know that you are their advocate. Once again, choose what applies in the parentheses to communicate effectively that you are for him and not against him. Say something like the following:

> "I think you're an amazing person and I (love, admire, care for) you. I'm glad you're my (spouse, parent, son or daughter, roommate, brother-in-Christ, friend, in-law, co-worker, etc.). I appreciate that you're (dependable, diligent, dedicated, determined, generous, passionate, responsible, etc.) when it comes to your (school, work, kids, grandchildren, parents, ministry, etc.). And I'm proud of you for that."

Confess Sin to Take Responsibility

Once you have affirmed your love and appreciation then take responsibility and confess what you have done to contribute to the conflict. By being honest and humble about your own sin first, you can demonstrate proper behavior and defuse the situation. Through your humble apology you tear down walls of defensiveness, pride, and self-preservation. God will lift you up for your obedience to humble yourself without making excuses. Take responsibility for what you did to contribute to the conflict after understanding their pain, perspective, and personality with words like,

> "Lately, I've done a lot of thinking and I can understand how you felt (rejected, unprotected, discouraged, unaccepted, unappreciated, or unheard) by me. I want to apologize for the way I (acted selfish, pulled away, put up a wall, put you down, lashed out in anger, made fun of you, ignored you, condemned you with my thoughts, interfered with your relationship, haven't supported your dream or been there for you emotionally, physically, or spiritually, etc.) I never meant to hurt you and I'm truly sorry. I want you to feel safe and secure and be able to trust me. Will you please forgive me?"

Confess your sin, because God promises to heal you when you do (James 5:16). Keep in mind that healing may not come right away. In fact, if for some reason the person begins to attack you verbally, avoid becoming defensive and angry. Nod in agreement as they share. Resist running away if they lash out with angry words. Try not to make excuses or cast blame. Instead, hold your tongue. Bite it if you have to! STOP to hear their heart.

Be in prayer for wisdom and discernment as they share. Listen for what they are feeling, which is not always the words that they say. Consider gently saying, "I want to hear what you have to say. Can you please be gentle with me?" Intimidation, anger, and threats will no longer work to control the relationship when you know who you are in Christ, which I share in the next and final chapter *Determine Your Identity*. Do not react to threats. Stay calm. Acknowledge what the person is saying to you whether you believe the accusation is completely accurate. Even if they responded out of false information that you need to clarify later with truth, first find common ground. Acknowledge that you heard their heart, empathize with their pain, and take responsibility for any part of the conflict you may have caused, whether intentional or unintentional. Do not be defensive or rude or let your mind go to unkind thoughts.

Tell the Truth with Thanksgiving

Express truth in love to promote maturity and build up the body of Christ. Unless we rely on God's truth we become unlovable through the deception of the one who schemes for our destruction. The devil is a liar. Satan uses people, but they are not our enemy. The devil is our adversary. In John 8:44 we read, *"The devil was a murderer from the beginning, not holding to the truth, for there is no truth in him. When he lies, he speaks his native language, for he is a liar and the father of lies."* Unlovable people are entrapped by wrong thinking that the devil has conveyed through messages inflicted by hurt people. Unlovable people carry the burden of their false beliefs every day. Try to discover the lie they believe. They may think you are blocking their goal to achieve success, peace, or unity. Determine if they are reacting from a place of protection for themselves or someone else.

We do people a disservice when we fail to tell them the truth of how their behavior is impacting themselves and others. In their helpful book *Safe People,* Dr. Cloud and Dr. Townsend explain that we are not to just support people through words of encouragement and praise, but to be honest with them to build their character. Jesus even told the church leaders that He had something against them. In the same way, we tell people what might be unpleasant, and at worse hurt their pride, but it won't harm them. To protect people from self-destructiveness and blindness, we must confront by being calm, confident, and controlled. [14] God says,

> If someone is caught in a sin, you who are spiritual should restore him gently. But watch yourself, or you also may be tempted. Carry each other's burdens, and in this way you will fulfill the law of Christ. If anyone thinks he is something when he is nothing, he deceives himself (Galatians 6:1-3).

Communicate the truth of how his or her behavior impacts you with humility, knowing you could easily fall into that same temptation or sin that they struggle with or another sin equally as bad from God's holy perspective. First, speak truth in love by reminding the difficult person that you are thankful for them. Just like Paul did in his Epistles to the church, he thanked God for those he rebuked. Although you may not feel thankful, God is using this person to grow you up in Christ. You will be maturing and becoming sanctified through this conversation. You may not do it perfectly, but be confident that you will continue to grow each time you step out in faith to be honest. Say something like the following:

"I'm thankful to have you in my life. And I want to be honest with you. I've learned that it's better to speak truth in love to become mature than not say anything at all, which leads to destruction. You probably don't even know that I feel (rejected, unprotected, unsafe, uncomfortable, betrayed) when you (put me down, watch porn, use drugs, drink, lie, yell, call me names, criticize me, miss work or

school, spend money we don't have, fail to follow through on a
commitment, etc.)."

Pay attention to their response to determine the lie they believe. Do
they trust you are for them and not against them? Do they believe God
loves them? What goal do they believe you are blocking? Do they
believe that the things of this world will fill the void in their heart? Are
they lacking in wisdom? Once you determine the lie, say something
like this:

"It sounds like you believe _____, but the truth is (I love you,
God loves you, or share any transforming truth from the next
chapter or from the list on pages 217-218 or one of the truths that
ministered to your heart in the previous pages)."

Share the truth as it relates to "us" as a team. Avoid "you"
statements that cast judgment. For example, you might say, "Nothing
can separate us from the love of Jesus. When we put our trust in Him
He will guide and direct our path." Or "When we humble ourselves to
God He will lift us up with resurrection power to conquer our sin." Or
"When we obey God we demonstrate our love for Him and He shows
Himself to us." Transform your relationship by speaking the truth in
love. It's our responsibility to do whatever it takes to penetrate the heart
of every person with God's truth, whether they believe or not. People
might be offended. As we share we risk that the unbeliever may not
understand spiritual matters, they may respond in anger, or reject us
completely, but it's worth the risk. God can use the conversation to
bring them to repentance and at the very minimum plant the mustard
seed of faith. The benefits outweigh the losses.

Communicating the powerful Word of God destroys the stronghold
of the enemy. You will become more mature and Christ-like when you
proclaim truth with courage and confidence. Consider sharing the
acrostic STOP or any of the Transforming Truths. As you speak truth,
use Scripture as your foundation, but avoid accusing or condemning the
person. Instead express God's Word from a heart of compassion to be

heard. Although they may be unaware of the fact that you are speaking God's Word, it will not return void, but will accomplish what God desires (Isaiah 55:11). Just as effective as sharing the truth when having a difficult conversation, you can share the truth outside of conflict.

Say What You Want with a Solution

Clarify your goals for unity, harmony, and trust in the relationship. Communicate your goal to protect the person and that you want your heart, mind, and body to be protected as well. Be intentional to communicate what you want. Unless we say what we want no one will know. Remember the person cannot read your mind, only your body language. I recommend using the following as a guide to say what you want for the relationship:

> "I want us to feel (close, protected, safe, secure, accepted, respected, encouraged, appreciated, etc.). I want us to have (peace, joy, security, freedom, success)."

You might need to remind the person how you have contributed to the relationship. Often we take people for granted and forget what they do for us. This next step is a gentle reminder to communicate how you enjoy serving them and how you want them to contribute. Try to focus on what you want as opposed to what you don't want. When you focus on the negative people feel condemned. Say something like,

> "I just need to let you know that in order for us to have a good relationship we both need to contribute. The way that I contribute is by (providing financial support, transportation, a safe and comfortable environment, cooking meals, the beautiful clothes you wear, encouragement, emotional support, praying for you, opportunities to participate in activities, etc.). The way I want you to contribute to our relationship is by (thanking me when I fix you a meal, giving me hugs, being honest, staying faithful, being clean

<u>and sober, doing your chores, being a good steward of our financial resources, calling me back, doing your homework, etc.).</u>"

This direct conversation has transformed relationships! Communicating that you want to contribute to the relationship and that you are a team will connect you with that person. Think of every relationship as a team effort. Build them up with words of encouragement and clearly state the benefits to the relationship and the losses or consequence if needed.

"We're a team. I accept you for who you are, but I don't agree with what you're doing right now. Your choices are impacting me. I still love you and I want you to know that I believe in you. There are blessings when we do the right thing, but when we don't there is a loss of (<u>respect, privileges, health, freedom, security, opportunities</u>). Your choice has brought the consequence of _____ until you can _____. I love you and I want to protect you from continuing down a path of destruction."

This would be a good time to set up goals if they haven't been established for the relationship. Consider working through this book together, admitting to him or her that you can be unlovable. Express to the person that you want the best for your relationship. And always remember your battle is not against flesh and blood, but the enemy in the heavenly realms. God warns, *"Be self-controlled and alert. Your enemy the devil prowls around like a roaring lion looking for someone to devour" (1 Peter 5:8)*. Satan wants to destroy you and the people in your realm of influence. As you can see, over the years Satan has come against me, but I can rejoice. God is victorious! He has won the battle.

STOP to See God at Work

I thought *how could we be in the same cycle again?*

Friction mounted with my teenagers as my husband and I remained bitter toward one another. Mark and I were divided on a decision he made regarding our teenage daughter. Without consulting me, my husband took away my daughter's car when we discovered that she broke our rule to abstain from sexual relations.

My husband wanted to protect Kylie from getting hurt and being disrespected by her boyfriend. At the same time, I wanted to protect my daughter. In fact, I projected my fears of my own mistakes onto her. Although I calmly shared all my concerns with Kylie, she wouldn't listen to me. She insisted on becoming sexually involved, even if it meant giving up her car. She did not want us to block her goal of what she thought was love and face the possibly of losing her boyfriend.

Kylie moved out and I took matters into my own hands to ensure that my daughter wouldn't go down the same path that I did, becoming dependent and obligated to her boyfriend, and the possibility of having an unplanned pregnancy. I went behind my husband's back to arrange for my parents to co-sign on a car loan.

Angry with me, my husband felt betrayed and disrespected. He believed that I prevented her from moving back home sooner, which she eventually did after six months. In the meantime, Mark and I were at a breaking point. I mentioned separation before he left on vacation with our boys. It was a vacation that I wasn't invited on. Rejected and betrayed, I chalked it up to one more thing against him.

Focused on the computer screen in front of me, I decided this would be *my* time to write without interruptions. At a loss for words, my mind raced with thoughts of separation and the steps I needed to take to prepare.

Not wanting to be outside God's will, the Holy Spirit nudged me to fast and pray for wisdom. Confident that God would clearly guide and direct my path, I trusted Him for the answer. Each day that I humbled myself before God, waiting patiently to hear His still quiet voice, God brought me a precious hummingbird to sit on the string of lights hanging from my patio cover. I rested in the loving arms of my heavenly Daddy. I felt His presence and heard His still quiet voice through His creation, reading His Word, and seeking Him with all my heart.

Gently God began to convict me of my sin.

In leadership at our church, I decided to call the Small Group Coordinator to step down from my position for a period of time. On the phone, I told John the reason for my decision. John said bluntly, "Kirsten, you should consider putting your book and faith coaching aside to focus on your family and submit to your husband. As his wife you should try to win him over with a gentle and quiet spirit."

"What?" my heart sank, defensively I said, "I *do* focus on my husband and family. I'm so close to being done with this book that I shouldn't have to set it aside."

I was mad. A lump formed in the back of my throat as I held back tears. I thought *why did I have to be the one to* give *up my dreams? Mark's the one who has the anger problem. Why should I submit to him? God's Word says to submit to one another.*

After we ended our conversation, I cried out to God, "Is this what you want? Am I supposed to give up *my* book? Am I supposed to submit to my husband when he doesn't even respect me?"

In the stillness of the moment I sensed God tell me to lay down the book. It wasn't *my* book; it was *His*.

It was hard to be obedient to sacrifice my dreams, even for a short period of time. But how could I tell people how to love the unlovable when I couldn't love my *own* husband? God guided me as I trusted Him. I needed help. Researching experts on the subject of relationships and seeking God for wisdom through His Word, I cried out for His mercy.

God showed me the servant-heart of Jesus washing His disciple's dirty feet. I questioned, *Is that what* you *want Lord? Am I supposed to wash my husband's feet? And while I'm at it, should I wash Connor and Cameron's feet too?*

Did I trust that God loved me and that He wanted the best for me? Was I willing to serve my family joyfully, to humble myself, and sacrifice my dreams? Equipped with more understanding of what it meant to serve by looking at Jesus' example, I anticipated that things would be better when my husband returned, but they weren't.

I waited for Mark to make the first attempt to reconcile.

He never did.

Finally, after going to my knees before God, I humbled myself before my husband, apologized for my disrespect, and took responsibility for going behind his back to buy our daughter a car. To my surprise, Mark did not receive my apology. He stood up rehashing the past, blaming me, and accusing me of running away from our problems.

Fed-up with his inability to have a respectful conversation, I sensed my next step. Calmly, I explained to my husband that I would be filing for separation, because he continued to lash out in anger and not take responsibility. That day I felt God lead me to a Christian attorney to pay the retainer fee and begin the official separation process.

That's when God intervened.

Out of desperation, Mark reached out to his closest friend, mentor, and accountability partner. Doug asked if we would meet with him and his wife. When we did, they asked me to hold off on filing an official separation for a week. I considered that God was leading me through them. I thought, *one week. I guess I can do that.* The next day I put a hold on the paperwork, although I still had a hard heart. I wanted to run in the opposite direction from my husband, but I was open to what God wanted me to do.

Mark and I committed to our friends, Doug and BJ, to read the Bible and pray together each morning. Although for years we knew that reading God's Word together was essential for our marriage, pride and fear kept us from doing it. As we read and prayed together, we both tried to avoid accusing one another, but one day I pointed out a verse where he fell short. This caused Mark to lash out in anger and defensiveness.

My mind raced with negative thoughts, wanting to move forward with the paperwork to separate. I met with BJ privately and said to her, "I can't do it. I can't handle his anger." Calmly she showed me the verse in James to consider my trials as pure joy, that the testing of my faith will develop perseverance so that I can become mature and complete, not lacking anything (James 1:2-4). She assured me that God would reward my obedience.

Sitting in her living room I resisted the devil and the temptation to run away. Literally, I wanted to yell at BJ, *"You don't understand! You don't have a husband like mine!"* Instead, I prayed. I submitted to God. I cried out silently for Him to help me not storm out of her house. As I humbled myself to God, I experienced His strength and resurrection power to overcome my anger. I reminded myself, moment by moment, to STOP.

Mark and I continued to meet with Doug and BJ every week for about six weeks. They heard the cries of our hearts and taught us to listen and validate one another. They pointed out that both of us were in pain, feeling unloved, discounted, and unsupported. We had been so focused on our own pain that we failed to see the pain we were inflicting on the other.

Meeting with Doug and BJ allowed us to witness a respectful relationship with healthy dialogue. This made me realize why being equally yoked in close fellowship with other believers is essential. We learn from one another. God used our spiritual sister and brother to teach us and hold us accountable as well as to fervently pray for us. Through the process God began to chip away at our stone hearts until there was a breakthrough.

One Saturday morning Mark agreed to sit outside on a beautiful warm September day. Grateful that he was willing to give up the comfort of sitting inside, I expressed my sincere appreciation. With my grateful attitude I noticed his demeanor change. After we read the Bible and prayed together we shared our hearts. By asking questions we gained understanding to the source of our pain. We recognized how our perspectives were different and some of our problems were caused by our diverse personalities. For the first time, there was a desire for me to truly *know* my husband and what makes him tick, instead of resenting him and focusing on my pain.

Outside on that sunny day, God tested me. Would I practice what I preached? Listening to Mark, I heard his pain. He said he felt wounded and unsafe with me. He didn't trust that I loved him. As he shared I saw him as a hurt little boy and God's precious child. In our lawn chairs we sat across from one another, we shared what we wanted for the relationship, and our goals to protect one another and the children. My heart softened toward him. I scooted my chair closer. I leaned over to hold his face and told him I loved him. I kissed him and held him for the first time in a long time.

Mark sighed with relief and held me tight.

No longer afraid of my husband and his harshness, I silently prayed to God *I'm trusting You with my heart, I'm submitting to You, Lord, so that You will empower me to submit to my husband and trust him.* Tears streamed down my face. I completely surrendered my life to Jesus and gave my heart to my husband. I wrapped my arms around him with complete freedom out of obedience to God. My hard heart softened.

We continued to practice the discipline of getting up at 5:30 to read the Bible and pray for our marriage and our children. On the few days that we sacrificed our time together for another commitment, or due to laziness, we suffered and our relationship struggled. Fortunately, we recognized the enemy as the one who caused dissension and we became more faithful and diligent to lift one another up in prayer, remembering our battle is not against flesh and blood, but against the evil forces in the heavenly realms (Ephesians 6:12).

For years I had believed the deception that my husband was my enemy. Now I believe the truth that my husband is my life long partner, my spiritual leader, and my friend. Even when he stumbles and doesn't get it right, I hold my thoughts captive to what's right, true, and pure by thinking on God's promises and praying for him. To obey God my husband reads the Bible to me and we pray together. Often I tell my husband how grateful I am that he loves me and that he washes me with the Word of God to be holy and blameless, emphasizing that I want to be the best wife and mother (Ephesians 4:25-27). Firsthand, we have witnessed the power of reading the Holy Scriptures together as our relationship has been transformed.

Opposites do attract for a reason. We complement one another. In those areas that we stumble, we are there to show grace, compassion, acceptance, and encourage one another with a gentle reminder. Initially, by *my* obedience and example to submit to my husband I have seen him submit to me, to serve and honor me in ways I could never have imagined. Often I receive a text message that tells me I'm adored and cherished. Not only that, he faithfully vacuums the house each week. And for me I hold my thoughts captive and serve my family joyfully. Over the next year and a half God brought me to a deeper understanding of the transforming truths that I share in this book that took my relationships to a whole new level of intimacy.

Sometimes it can be hard to change old patterns that are comfortable. For years I fell back into the same habits. Going back to that familiar place, maybe it's how I felt as a child— abandoned, alone, and filled with the shame of not being seen. Nestled in my place of isolation, comfortable in my condemnation, I pulled away. I hid behind my computer to manipulate more words on a page or I went to the coffee shop where they knew my name. Where do you go? Do you hide behind social media or a glass of wine or the pantry to snack or the mall to shop? Where is your place of self-loathing or justification? We can even appear righteous hiding behind our Bibles instead of restoring our broken relationships. Although I knew what I was supposed to do, it took me so long to humble myself to do it.

From a young age I never had proper attachment toward my family. Taking the life of my first child through abortion, I emotionally detached like my parents. The date rape and each sexual experience caused me to guard my heart. Married to Mark, I never fully committed to him. I secretly eloped with the idea that I could secretly divorce. I kept the backdoor open to leave. I needed to close the door, to be committed. I needed to obey God no matter what Mark did or didn't do, and continue to seek God with all my heart believing God had plans to prosper us. What Mark did was between him and God. I was only responsible for my relationship with Jesus, not his.

Too often we pretend to be a peacemaker and live a lie, which forfeits our freedom. Until we learn that to be set free is to speak the truth in love. Believe that when we are honest that God "*is able to do immeasurably more than all we ask or imagine, according to his power that is at work within us*" *(Ephesians 3:20)*.

Did you catch that promise? His power is at work within you. He will do immeasurably more in you and through you than you can even imagine. Have you imagined how you want your relationship to be? You don't receive if you don't ask. Ask with the right motives and take refuge in knowing that God loves you and has plans to prosper you when you seek Him with all of your heart (James 4:3, Jeremiah 29:11-13). Then, no matter what happens you will be secure knowing that you were obedient to God. No matter what happens you can be confident that God has allowed it for a purpose to prosper you. And no matter what happens you know your identity, taught in the following and final chapter.

Faithful Father, prior to laying my gift at the altar of your throne of grace I want to be reconciled to _____. Please help me to no longer procrastinate doing what I know I should do. Instead, help me to put off falsehood and speak truth in love, so that we will in all things grow up to become mature in Christ. I am the salt of the earth and I refuse to be thrown out and trampled underfoot by not obeying you. Let me speak truth boldly and confidently and restore him/her gently. Help me to watch myself that I may not be tempted in any way to think that I am better. Help me discern the lies of the enemy that I may rebuke the devil with the transforming truth that will set _____ free. Go before me to prepare his/her heart to receive my message and give me the words to say to communicate love, grace, and healing. Be glorified through me as I speak truth in Jesus faithful and mighty name. Amen. Matthew 5:23-24; James 4:17; Ephesians 4:15, 25; Matthew 5:13; John 8:44; Galatians 6:1-3.

GOD'S TRANSFORMING TRUTH
Express truth in love to become mature: "Speaking the truth in love, we will in all things grow up into Him who is the Head, that is, Christ... Therefore each of you must put off falsehood and speak truthfully to his neighbor, for we are all members of one body" (Ephesians 4:15, 25).

QUESTION TO PONDER
What lie is causing dissension in your relationship?

TAKE ACTION
Take the hand of your difficult person and speak truth with gentleness, humility, and confidence to promote maturity and build up the body of Christ.

Chapter Twelve

Determine Your Identity

Christ in you, the hope of glory.
Colossians 1:27

For years my happiness was defined by whether my husband, children, and other people were happy with me. My self-worth was intertwined with what others thought or said or did. Once you understand your identity comes from Christ, your perspective changes. When people come against you, you can have confidence. Knowing God loves you, you can trust that God is allowing the conflict for a purpose. In fact, conflict becomes an avenue to communicate your message of hope. Your pilgrimage won't be easy as a Christian. As you know, there are many unlovable people who will accuse, ostracize, and betray you, in and out of the church, but their feelings or words or actions will never determine who you are.

As we conclude our time together in this final chapter on how to love unlovable people, my prayer is that you are encouraged to apply God's truth to your difficult relationship. Meditate on God's Word and let this chapter equip you to become confident in your identity, purpose, and inheritance in CHRIST. For you are His witness as it is written, *"To them God has chosen to make known among the Gentiles the glorious riches of this mystery, which is Christ in you, the hope of glory" (Col. 1:27).* Christ lives in you to bring the hope of heaven to the hurting. Consider using the following as a guide to minister to the hearts of those who feel unloved and unlovable. They need to know the truth to set them free to live the abundant life God has for them.

You are Created in God's Image

You were created by Christ to reflect the image of Christ. According to God, your ancestors never crawled out of the sea, randomly appeared, or evolved from an ape. No, instead you were specifically created for the purpose to be in relationship with your Creator and to bring others into a right relationship with Him. You are valuable! Fearfully and wonderfully made, God sees you and knows you. There is nowhere you can go apart from His love. Your insecurities are gone as you delight in who you are in Christ. Never doubt that you are capable to do what God has called you to do, since He promises that you have the mind of Christ and can do all things through Him who strengthens you. Christ has given you a new identity when you invited Him into your life to reign and rule. Surrendering all that you are; all that you have; and all that you do will transform you into a new creation in Christ (Genesis 1:27, John 1:14, Psalm 139:8-14, 1 Cor. 2:16, Phil. 4:13, 2 Cor. 5:17).

When your identity is in Christ unlovable people have no power over you. No longer do you have to react to what people say or do. Self-worth comes from what God says about you, not people. In fact, your identity should not be about your career, how much money you make, or where you live; or what school you attend; or what your kids accomplish; or how tight your abs, large your chest, or successful your ministry. None of that matters! Your identity is not about performance or perfection or position. Instead, everything you do and say becomes a means to bless God and others. Even building an empire of wealth has little significance compared to building the kingdom of God. In fact, when blessed with wealth it's all about blessing others.

With Christ the old is gone! Do you believe that? Through the process of sanctification and purification, becoming Christ-like, you are changing into that person you want to be. You can love the unlovable. You can see people from the heart of God. It's no longer about you or me. Life is about ministering God's grace, truth, and love. No longer reacting from a place of pain, you have purpose to reflect God's glory.

You are Healed for a Purpose

Talking to the chosen people of Israel, the nation in which God chose to bring the Messiah, God wrote the following scripture through the Prophet Isaiah:

> *The Spirit of the Sovereign Lord is on me, because the Lord has anointed me to preach good news to the poor. He has sent me to bind up the brokenhearted, to proclaim freedom for the captives and release from darkness for the prisoners, to proclaim the year of the Lord's favor and the day of vengeance of our God, to comfort all who mourn (Isaiah 61:1-2).*

Jesus read these words in the synagogue to fulfill the scriptures. Today, He anoints you with the power of the Holy Spirit to bring the same message of hope and healing. Many hurt people feel hopeless, since the enemy wants to isolate, intimidate, and interrogate by whispering lies of unworthiness. This is precisely why I shared not only my story, but also the stories of others who experienced deep pain and sorrow. The past pages contained testimonies of victims who became victorious through Christ, healed from a life of violence, addiction, and sexual immorality to minister to the hearts of God's people.

For the first time you may have remembered offenses you have buried. Maybe you were sexually molested or violently assaulted or ended a life through abortion. If you are experiencing shame and hopelessness, Jesus wants to take that away. He wants to heal your heart, to make you whole, and give you freedom from all your pain and guilt and shame through His truth. Jesus offers healing. You have a choice to make. Will you accept His healing or continue to cast blame on others? There's a story in the Bible that illustrates this point. Jesus saw a paralytic man lying on a mat near a pool of water that was known to heal. He asked him, *"Do you want to get well?"* Instead of the man answering yes, he gave excuses and blamed people for going ahead of him. Then Jesus said to him, *"Get up! Pick up your mat and walk"* *(John 5:6-9).* Finally, the man stopped complaining and got up and walked. He believed the words of Jesus and was healed.

What is your mat? Is it the memory of abuse or using drugs, alcohol, or sex to bury your pain? What has you paralyzed and crippled? Jesus says, *"Get up and walk."* You are healed! Live the life of freedom that God has for you. Emotional, mental, spiritual, and physical healing is yours. Sometimes complete healing can happen right away, and other times it's a gradual process. Either way, you can be sure that God came to rescue you from the bondage of the evil that was done against you and that you have committed against others. God never intended for you to stay broken and bruised, but instead He binds-up your broken heart to bring you wholeness as His beloved. Isaiah 53:5 says this about Jesus,

> *He was pierced for our transgressions, He was crushed for our iniquities; the punishment that brought us peace was upon Him, and by His wounds we are healed.*

You can be sure that complete healing will certainly come when we are resurrected with a new body in heaven where there is no more pain or sorrow or suffering (Psalm 103:3, Revelation 21:4). Call on the name of Jesus to heal you. With healing comes purpose to share the good news with others that will set them free from the bondage of their pain and shame. *"What the enemy intended for harm God intended for good to accomplish the saving of many lives" (Genesis 50:20).*

You are Righteous by His Blood

To be in right relationship we must expose our sin to Jesus, to the one who died for that sin, who paid the price for our disobedience. He promises to cleanse us,

> *But if we walk in the light as He is in the light, we have fellowship with one another, and the blood of Jesus Christ His Son cleanses us from all sin. If we say that we have no sin, we deceive ourselves, and the truth is not in us. If we confess our sins, He is faithful and just to forgive us our sins and to cleanse us from all unrighteousness (1 John 1:7-9).*

Your confession brings purification from the One who covers you by His blood. As you take the time to be sensitive to the Holy Spirit in prayer and by reading your Bible, God will convict you of your sin. Bringing that sin into the light and presence of God you acknowledge your wrong behavior and thoughts. You will no longer justify the sin, but are appalled and repulsed by it, knowing that your sin hurts the heart of God. When the Holy Spirit lives inside a believer who continues to deliberately sin, the Spirit is grieved. God cannot tolerate sin. He is a righteous and holy God. If you're unsure of what grieves the Holy Spirit look at this list from Ephesians 4:30-32 that says,

Do not grieve the Holy Spirit of God, with whom you were sealed for the day of redemption. Get rid of all bitterness, rage and anger, brawling and slander, along with every form of malice. Be kind and compassionate to one another, forgiving each other, just as in Christ God forgave you.

Do you have bitterness, fear, doubt, selfish motives, a negative attitude, slander, pride, or a rebellious spirit? If yes, then grieve your double-mindedness. Go before God to confess your sin to be cleansed of all unrighteousness and make restitution with the Holy Spirit in you. It's that easy! Don't beat yourself up if you fall. Just confess the sin and God will do the rest. He promises to purify you. God wants your body to be cleansed of all unwanted and ungodly thoughts, desires, and practices. You are His dwelling place, sealed with the Holy Spirit, to be aligned with the Father's will. His perfect and pleasing will is to represent the love of Jesus to save His people. To be a vessel of God's love you must banish sin from your temple. In the following testimony read how God is using Kent's obedience to deliver prisoners from darkness.

Kent's Testimony

Kent felt unlovable. It started when he was four. An older boy and girl in his neighborhood molested Kent, which took him down a road of allowing other kids to bully and abuse him physically, emotionally, and sexually. Although Kent knew his parents loved him, they gave him the message that something was wrong with him, like a disabled child his mother coddled him, frustrated that he couldn't protect and stand up for himself. His parents had no idea their young boy had been molested and over the years he was too ashamed to tell them.

Desperate to be accepted by his peers, 17 year old Kent gravitated toward another boy who was an outcast like him, someone else who carried secret shame. To prove his loyalty and gain acceptance with his new friend, Kent followed through on the boy's plan to kill his father and girlfriend.

Serving a life sentence for a double murder, Kent battled a horrible illness that had all the markers of AIDS. The night before his test results were to come back, Kent cried out on what appeared to be his deathbed, asking God to heal him. In return he promised to commit his life to follow God. The results came back negative for HIV, and within two days the chronic symptoms that had persisted disappeared.

The miraculous transformation fueled Kent's commitment to serve and obey God, and by doing so God has blessed him. He wakes up at four o'clock each morning to read his Bible, to meditate on God's Word, and to pray for the many people in the prison. Kent is in constant prayer during the day and because of his desire to please God, he is sensitive to the still small voice that guides and directs his path. Often times Kent has trusted the nudging of the Holy Spirit to move from one location to another in the dangerous prison yard. His obedience has saved his life from violent outbreaks that have occurred in the very spot where Kent once stood moments before.

God is using Kent in a powerful way to encourage inmates to stay committed in their relationship with God, to not straddle the fence, but to choose wisely who and what they will become a slave to. He counsels Christians to distance themselves from evil to follow the One true living God and to obey, even in the small things like grumbling and complaining in the food line. Kent is doing kingdom work in the prison. His life reminds me of the following promise from God to be blessed when we follow His ways instead of the world's ways:

Blessed is the one who does not walk in step with the wicked or stand in the way that sinners take or sit in the company of mockers, but whose delight is in the law of the Lord, and who meditates on his law day and night. That person is like a tree planted by streams of water, which yields its fruit in season and whose leaf does not whither— whatever they do prospers (Psalm 1:1-3).

God prospered Kent in prison with overwhelming peace in the presence of his enemies as he surrendered his life to God every moment of the day, trusting that God loves him and will protect him, as he obeys and delights in the Lord. Even violent gang members respect Kent for his faith because his walk reflects his talk. If he was double-minded, faking his Christianity by going to the prison chapel to avoid evil inmates, he would suffer beatings, rape, and possible death. Kent was put to the test many times. God has honored his obedience by fulfilling His promise in Proverbs 16:7, *"When a man's ways are pleasing to the Lord, He makes even his enemies live at peace with him."*

By the grace of God you are made righteous. No matter what you have done you are forgiven and cleansed of all immorality. God's Word says, *"For Christ died for sins once for all, the righteous [Jesus] for the unrighteous [humanity], to bring you to God. He was put to death in the body but made alive by the Spirit" (1 Peter 3:18).* The Holy Spirit will equip you to be righteous. Not on your own accord, but by Jesus' death and resurrection you have the power of God in you. Sin is dead. That's God's promise! *"There is now no condemnation for those who are in Christ Jesus, because through Christ Jesus the law of the Spirit of life set you free from the law of sin and death" (Romans 8:1).* You are free!

We no longer fight for the love of man when we grasp the love of Christ. Live to please Him alone. See yourself as a temple of God not to be defiled. When you see yourself as a treasure of the Lord, it will make a difference in the way you treat yourself and others. When you truly understand the undeserving grace of God you will extend that grace to those who hurt you.

The question is would someone identify you as a *little Christ*? That's what we want! Your identity, and mine, should be so closely knit to Jesus that people see Him in us. Do you glorify God with every person: rich or poor, straight or homosexual, gentle or hostile? When your identity is secure in Christ, you no longer have to prove you're right and they're wrong. Reflect the love of Jesus and speak truth in love. God will do the rest. Demonstrating the love of Christ, the Holy Spirit will convict the unlovable. With conviction comes confession that leads to becoming a new creation. Remember to reflect a heart of compassion to the unlovable rather than condemnation as Christ has done for you. Your reward is the abounding joy and peace that you experience when you do the right thing when it seems impossible.

You are Included in God's Family

The Father chose you! You are His precious and favored child. You have been adopted into God's family. Adoption can be a long and arduous process that can cost a tremendous amount of money. Our Father in heaven paid a great price for you to become a member of His family. He gave His one and only Son to die for you. Jesus poured out His blood to include you into His royal family. You are the Father's beloved, a prince or princess, and co-heir to the throne of Christ. Due to His great love for you, God never intended for you to live this life alone and isolated. Instead, God calls the church the body of Christ, a spiritual family, to do life together. That's why I wrote this book for you. Each member of our spiritual family has gifts, talents, life experiences, pain, and passion to be used for the purpose to love God's people. To do that, He plans for you to get involved with the church.

The people in church are imperfect, just like you and me. In fact, there are many unlovable people in the pews, since we have different levels of maturity. That's precisely why we speak truth in love to build up the body of Christ. We need one another *"as iron sharpens iron, so one man sharpens another" (Proverbs 27:17)*. Being yoked with believers will allow encouragement, accountability, the practice of patience, understanding into God's Word, and prayer support to conquer your old life.

There's good reason why God tells you to be equally yoked with believers. Life becomes more complicated when you have unbelieving friends and family who tempt you in areas of sinful behavior. You are to live in the world, but not become tempted by the ways of the world. You are to love unbelievers, to serve them, to minister to their hearts, and even speak truth in love with the purpose to save them from destruction. But do not allow those friendships to pull you away from God. If you struggle with sin, then limit your time with those who cause you to stumble. You may need to take some time away from a relationship until you can stand firm in your faith to withstand temptation. Let me clarify, if you are married to an unbeliever, the Bible is clear not to divorce your spouse for that reason. God wants to use you to be the love of Jesus to win the unbeliever over to Christ by your gentle spirit (1 Cor. 7:13-14; 1 Peter 3:1).

The body of Christ is crippled and maimed without you. You have gifts and talents that God has given to you to contribute to your spiritual family. Over the years our church family came alongside us to be the hands and feet of Jesus with encouragement, meals, childcare, prayer, and financial support during Connor's battle with leukemia. During our marriage struggles and the challenge to raise four teenagers we received godly counsel. The will of God is that we live, breathe, and function as one body in perfect unity. In fact, Jesus prayed to His Father, *"May they [the church] be brought to complete unity to let the world know that you sent me and have loved them even as you have loved me" (John 17:23).* We do life together to glorify God.

You are a Servant to Love

Slow down to love. God wants us to have peace of mind, but many of us don't know what that looks like. Busy can appear productive, successful, and a life with purpose, but often it's at the expense of our relationships. With over-committed schedules we can be unlovable. Activities like work, volunteering, cleaning house, and shopping can be meaningful, important, and even necessary areas of life. The question to ask is *Am I too busy to spend time with my loved ones? Am I using my gifts and talents to glorify God and give others hope? Am I at peace in all my relationships?*

For every new project you commit to, you give up something else, usually less time doing what you love and spending less time with those you love. If every person was committed to serve their spouse and children first, this world would be a better place. Slow down to evaluate your life. Consider that the people in your life may be jealous or feel abandoned. Are you ignoring them as you serve others or are you busy running errands? Search your heart, check your motives, and make a list of all your activities. Eliminate what takes you away from being in right relationship with God and the people placed in your life.

With a heart of humility extend undeserved acts of kindness to overcome the deception ensnared by the evil one. Humble yourself to draw near to the presence of God. With a heart of humility you will be able to smile and say a kind word to a scowling clerk who might have aching feet; at work encourage the disgruntled co-worker who may be concerned about his job; in your community love the military and police with a word of thanksgiving for the stress they and their families endure to keep us safe. Even if you get a speeding ticket, you can bless the officer! Every circumstance is an opportunity to minister the love of Jesus. Be willing and obedient to do what God has called you to do. As you follow Him you will see God at work. Who does He want you to serve today?

You are a Testimony of God's Power

God saved you to display His power among his people (Psalm 106:8). Think of Moses who delivered the ungrateful Israelites out of bondage and slavery from the Egyptians, not by his own strength, but by the power of God displayed through him. Through the miracles that God did, people believed and were saved (Exodus 14:31). When we share the miracles of God then He is glorified and people are saved. Determine your identity in Christ to reflect God's glory on earth.

Sometimes we have preconceived ideas of who is worthy of God's love. Watch out for the deception of pride. God will humble the proud. We saw this happen when God told Jonah to tell the wicked people of Nineveh to repent of their sins. Jonah refused. Prejudice against the powerful Assyrians, known for their atrocities against Israel, prevented Jonah from wanting God to save them. Instead he ran the opposite direction toward the west where he boarded a ship in the port of Joppa to sail to Tarshish, a place far away from these ungodly people. Yet God knows our comings and goings, and He would stop at nothing to get Jonah to share a message of mercy and hope to a people who despised Him.

Thrown overboard into the tumultuous waters of the Mediterranean Sea, God saved Jonah through a fish. Jonah spent three days in the slimy belly of a fish until he repented. In faith and by the power of God, Jonah walked through the city of Nineveh proclaiming God's judgment and wrath if the people refused to repent. Speaking truth out of obedience, Jonah turned the hearts of one hundred and twenty thousand people in the capital city of Assyria toward God.

We disobey God when we fail to share the reason for our hope. Jesus said, *"Go into all the world and preach the good news to all creation" (Mark 16:15)*. Pride kept Jonah from preaching the message of hope to a nationality of people who he thought should suffer. We must not judge who is worthy of God's message or who is not. God is righteous and just. He wants all to come to repentance, even the murderer in prison, the jihadist who has intentions to bring down democracy, the drug dealer who has children hooked on crystal meth, and the person who ripped apart a family by stealing the love of their life. In our daily interactions, how many times do we subconsciously decide who deserves to be saved? Instead, when given the opportunity, share the message of truth and watch God at work.

Saheed's Testimony

Consider that divine appointments happen throughout your day. Recently my car battery died. After I called for roadside assistance a polite Middle Eastern man greeted me at my front door. We walked out to my vehicle when the Holy Spirit nudged me to investigate his faith by commenting on the weather. I went on to say "God's creation is amazing," paying attention to his response. I concluded he was not a Christian by the way he ignored my comment as he worked on my car.

After a silent prayer for wisdom and for the Holy Spirit to guide my conversation, I blessed this man with God's truth. I proceeded to tell him how God is personal and He does miracles. I shared my testimony that God healed my son from leukemia and healed my marriage. Then I waited to hear his response. He proceeded to tell me he was a Muslim, but not practicing his faith. He shared how he escaped out of Iran to come to the United States several years ago and that he felt lucky that he was not indoctrinated into extreme Islam. I interjected, "Consider that it was not *luck*, but that it was the hand of God who saved you. God blessed you by bringing you to this country, to a place where you could be free to choose what religion you want to follow." He nodded, as he contemplated what I said.

With the conversation now focused on faith, I told him how I never knew until a few years ago that God loved me. I said, "God loves you and me so much that He sent his Son, Jesus, to die on a cross to take the punishment of all our sin." I went on to say, "I always knew that Jesus died on the cross, but I never knew He died for *me*." Then I asked, "Do you know that Jesus died for *you*?" He admitted he never heard that.

Most people know Jesus died on a cross, but they don't know that Jesus died for them. I informed the man that Jesus is alive and personal, that God speaks to us through the Bible like a love letter. He said that he wanted a Bible when I offered to give him one. While he replaced my battery I collected a Bible, my Faith Coach bookmark with seven promises from God, and information to attend my church with his family. This Muslim man beamed with joy as he expressed his sincere gratitude. Then the Holy Spirit nudged me to ask if he wanted to invite Jesus into his heart before he left for his next appointment. He said yes, and I praised God. We stood in my driveway as the angels in heaven rejoiced that this one man repented of his sin and surrendered his life to

Christ (Luke 15:7). God filled me with joy to know that my new brother was set free.

You are His witness of the good news of Jesus to those who are lost and gone astray. Share your testimony to bring hope and healing to those who are harassed and helpless, to set people free from their prison of pain and despair. The book of Revelation reveals that the enemy is conquered and overcome by the blood of Jesus and the word of your testimony (Revelation 12:11). Christ will use your testimony to conquer Satan and his demons that are out to destroy, deceive, and distract people from knowing their loving Father. God stopped at nothing to demonstrate His love for you through His humble and obedient Son. His actions said *I refuse to be separated from you for eternity. I will do whatever it takes to bring you into a right relationship with Me.* With outstretched arms on a wooden cross Jesus communicated His love for you. By the power and authority of Christ in you, open up your arms to embrace those who feel unloved to proclaim God's transforming truth to set them free.

I love you Lord. My identity is in you, Christ Jesus. CREATED in your image, I am fearfully and wonderfully made, and you are with me. Thank you for indwelling me with your Spirit to have the mind of Christ and that I can do all things through Him who strengthens me. I rejoice that I am a new creation HEALED by your wounds for a purpose. What the enemy intended for harm, you intend for good to accomplish the saving of many lives. I am RIGHTEOUS by your grace alone through the blood of Jesus. You have chosen me to be INCLUDED in your royal family as your precious child. You saved me from destruction that I may live with you one day in my heavenly home where there is no more pain or suffering. I am your SERVANT to preach the good news to the poor, to bind up the brokenhearted, proclaim freedom for the captives and release from darkness for the prisoners, to proclaim the Lord's favor, and to comfort all who mourn. Even my enemies will live at peace with me as I stop to live according to your transforming truths. I am a TESTIMONY of your love and power with Christ in me, the hope of your glory to love the unlovable. In Jesus' name I pray. Amen. Psalm 139:8-14; 1 Cor. 2:16; Phil. 4:13; Genesis 1:27, 2 Cor. 5:17; Genesis 50:20; Romans 8:1; Isaiah 61:1-2; Proverbs 16:7, Col. 1:27.

GOD'S TRANSFORMING TRUTH

Determine your identity in Christ to reflect God's glory on earth:
"Christ in you, the hope of glory." (Colossians 1:27)

QUESTION TO PONDER

What was the old you like, and how are you a new creation in Christ?

TAKE ACTION

Share your testimony of how you're a new creation in Christ, healed, righteous, and included in God's family to overcome the enemy and bring the hope of His glory.

God's Transforming Truths

Walk with Jesus to have authentic relationships: *"If we walk in the light, as He is in the light, we have fellowship with one another, and the blood of Jesus, His Son, purifies us from all sin" (1 John 1:7).*

Forgive to be set free to love: *Jesus said, "If you forgive men when they sin against you, your heavenly Father will also forgive you...If you hold to my teaching, you are really my disciples. Then you will know the truth, and the truth will set you free" (Matthew 6:14, John 8:31-32).*

Teach by example to reconcile people to God: *"He has committed to us the message of reconciliation. We are therefore Christ's ambassadors, as though God were making his appeal through us" (2 Cor. 5:19-20).*

Be motivated by a pure heart to see God: *"Blessed are the pure in heart, for they will see God" (Matthew 5:8).*

Proclaim your power to conquer fear: *"For God has not given us a spirit of fear, but of power and of love and of a sound mind" (2 Timothy 1:7NKJV).*

Overcome evil with blessing to receive a blessing: *"Do not repay evil with evil or insult with insult, but with blessing, because to this you were called so that you may inherit a blessing" (1 Peter 3:9).*

Ask God for wisdom who gives generously: *"If any of you lacks wisdom, you should ask God, who gives generously to all without finding fault, and it will be given to you. But when he asks he must believe and not doubt" (James 1:5-6).*

Establish the goal to protect to demonstrate love: *"Love always protects" (1 Cor. 13:7).*

STOP to handle anger to become righteous: *"Everyone should be quick to listen, slow to speak and slow to become angry, for man's anger does not bring about the righteous life that God desires" (James 1:19-20).*

SURRENDER to God to be lifted up: *"Submit yourselves, then, to God. Resist the devil, and he will flee from you. Come near to God and he will come near to you...Humble yourselves before the Lord, and he will lift you up" (James 4:7-8, 10).*

TRUST that God loves you and He will direct your path: *"Neither death nor life, neither angels nor demons, neither the present nor the future, nor any powers, neither height nor depth, nor anything else in all creation, will be able to separate us from the love of God that is in Christ Jesus our Lord" (Romans 8:38-39). "Trust in the Lord with all your heart and lean not on your own understanding; in all your ways acknowledge Him, and He will make your paths straight" (Proverbs 3:5-6).*

OBEY God to demonstrate love for Him and see Him at work: *"Whoever has my commands and obeys them, he is the one who loves me. He who loves me will be loved by my Father, and I too will love him and show myself to him" (John 14:21).*

PRAY to unleash God's power: *Jesus said, "If you remain in me and my words remain in you, ask whatever you wish, and it will be given you. This is to my Father's glory, that you bear much fruit, showing yourselves to be my disciples" (John 15:7-8).*

Take responsibility in order to be healed: *"Confess your sins to each other and pray for each other so that you may be healed" (James 5:16).*

Express truth in love to become mature: *"Speaking the truth in love, we will in all things grow up into Him who is the Head, that is, Christ" (Ephesians 4:15).*

Determine your identity in Christ to reflect God's glory on earth: *"Christ in you, the hope of glory" (Colossians 1:27).*

Twelve Action Steps

1. Meet Jesus at the well of your heart. He sees you. He knows you. He hears you. Listen to His sweet gentle voice. He loves you. Make the decision to invite Him into your pain.

2. Pour out your heart in a letter using the Steps to Forgive without giving it to the person. Out of obedience confess your sin of bitterness and say a prayer to forgive each person to be set free to love.

3. Write a list of ways you can demonstrate proper behavior to those who are watching you.

4. Confess your negative thoughts to God. With an attitude of gratitude make a list of all the positive qualities in your difficult person and make a point to speak words of appreciation.

5. Rise in the morning to put on the full armor of God with praise, prayer, and proclamation of His promises in the name of Jesus.

6. Ask the difficult person, "How do you feel most loved by me?" Discuss what you've learned in this chapter.

7. Be vulnerable. Share your past pain, perspectives, and personality with transparency to build trust. Ask questions to know and understand the hurt person.

8. Decide how to protect the mind, body, and spirit of the person you struggle with as well as yourself.

9. STOP to identify what you want for the relationship and establish an action plan on how to achieve your goals.

10. Humble yourself by apologizing for your contribution to the conflict.

11. Take the hand of your difficult person and speak truth with gentleness, humility, and confidence to promote maturity and build up the body of Christ.

12. Share your testimony of how you're a new creation in Christ, healed, righteous, and included in God's family to overcome the enemy and bring the hope of His glory.

12-Week Bible Study / Discussion Questions

Chapter One: Come Out of Hiding

1. Did you relate to any part of Kirsten's story? What are some of the ways you may be hiding from intimacy with God and others?
2. Read the story of the woman at the well in John 4:1-42. How can you relate to the Samaritan woman? How was she changed after she met Jesus at the well?
3. What is the benefit of walking in the light as promised in 1 John 1:7?
4. How have you been rejected? What are you ashamed of that restricts you from authentic relationships and prevents you from being the person God created you to be?
5. What does God say to your heart through Hebrews 12:1-3? Read Romans 10:9, have you confessed Jesus as Lord?

Chapter Two: Forgive to Be Set Free

1. How did Bill's testimony impact you? Why should you forgive? (Matt. 6:14; John 8:31-32; Luke 23:34, Matt. 18:21-22)
2. Read Joseph's story in Gen. 37, 39-50. What can we learn from Joseph's response to the betrayal of his brothers in Genesis 50:15-21?
3. Read Romans 8:28, what does God do when we love and follow Him?
4. Do you remember a situation when God has worked something for good that seemed horrible at the time?
5. What does God promise in James 4:7-10? Have you been double-minded?
6. Who do you need to forgive to be set free from the bondage of bitterness to be filled with God's peace and joy? Follow the steps to forgive outlined in the chapter. Did you say a prayer to forgive the people who hurt you?

Chapter Three: Teach by Example

1. How did Mel's testimony impact you? What are you teaching the people around you at work or at home through your behavior? How did your earthly father influence your view of your heavenly Daddy?
2. What are some of the ways Jesus teaches us proper behavior? Read John chapter 13:1-17, what does Jesus promise when we follow Him? How would you rate your level of commitment to following Christ?
3. Describe your prayer life? Read James 5:15, Matt. 18:19-20, 1 Tim. 2:1-4.

4. How do you demonstrate that you follow Christ according to John 13:34-35?
5. Could you relate to Kirsten's story about picking up dog poop? When did you demonstrate the love of Jesus when it seemed impossible and how did you feel afterwards?

Chapter Four: Motivated by a Pure Heart

1. What causes fights and quarrels according to James 4:1-3?
2. What does God's Word say about selfish ambition and pride according to Phil. 2:3-4? When have you experienced selfish ambition or vain conceit?
3. How do you overcome negative thoughts according to Phil. 4:8; 2 Cor. 10:4-5, Phil. 2:14-15? What are some positive qualities listed on page 71 that you can use to build up and encourage the unlovable person?
4. What are some of your thoughts and words that are reflecting the condition of your heart? What does God promise in Matthew 5:8?
5. What happens when you completely trust that God loves you? Look up Prov. 3:5-6, Jeremiah 17:7. How do you know God loves you?
6. What do you learn from looking at Abraham's life in Genesis 22? What does God promise when we obey according to John 14:21?

Chapter Five: Proclaim Your Power

1. What do you learn from observing Paul and Silas in Acts 16? On page 89, what are the steps to avoid anxiousness according to Phil. 4:4-7? What can you praise God for in your situation?
2. According to 2 Tim. 1:7 and 2 Peter 1:4 what has God given you? What must you do to receive God's power?
3. According to God's Word in Eph. 6:10-13, who is your battle against? What can you do to be prepared, pages 94-96?
4. What do the scriptures tell you about your power in Luke 10:17-20, Romans 5:5, Acts 1:8, Acts 3:16, Prov. 18:10, Acts 2:21, Psalm 91:11-14?
5. Why did God save you according to Psalm 106:8? How do you display God's power from the topics discussed in this chapter?

Chapter Six: Overcome Evil with Blessing

1. What is God's promise when you bless someone who is rude or mean to you according to 1 Peter 3:9, Matt. 25:40, and Gal. 5:16-23?

2. According to this chapter what are some ways to bless the unlovable? Why are unbelievers unable to understand what we say according to, John 8:43-45, 2 Cor. 4:4? What does the devil do according to John 8:44?
3. When did you bless someone who was cruel to you? What do you reap when you are kind in return, according to Galatians 6:8, Matt. 5:3-12?
4. In what ways do you and your difficult person feel most loved?

Chapter Seven: Wise-Up to Understand

1. How do we obtain wisdom according to Proverbs 11:2 and James 1:5-6?
2. How must you live according to Ephesians 5:15-16?
3. Read Psalm 139, how are you impacted by knowing that God knows you? Why should you desire to know the person you are in conflict with?
4. What insight did you gain from this chapter on your perspective verses the other person's perspective? (pages 122-125)
5. Determine your personality and their personality, how can you adapt?
6. Are you projecting someone onto your relationship?
7. After praying Psalm 139:23-24, has God revealed anything to you?

Chapter Eight: Establish the Goal to Protect

1. How does God protect your relationship with Him and others according to Matt. 22:37-39 and Exodus 20:1-17? What area do you struggle with? Bring your sin and shame into the light to be healed. Read 1 John 1:7-9.
2. Read 1 Cor. 13:7, who are you trying to protect and why?
3. Did you relate to Dottie or Patty's testimonies? What improper behaviors do you allow that separate people from you and God?
4. What goals have you established in the area of mind, body, and spirit?
5. Why should you protect yourself from sexual immorality according to 1 Cor. 6:18-20? How has the idea of the Holy Spirit living in you changed your life?

Chapter Nine: STOP to Handle Anger

1. How do you avoid anger from becoming a root of bitterness according to James1:19-20; Proverbs 29:11; Eph. 4:26-27; Psalm 37:8?
2. Read James 1:26-27, what does God consider to be worthwhile religion?
3. What are God's promises from the acrostic STOP on page 152?
4. What did you learn from Kenji and Charlene's testimony (2 Cor. 1:3-4)?

5. What are some of the blocked goals or fears that are causing conflict?
6. Read Psalm 1:1-3, Prov. 3:11-12, Romans 12:12, how do you do battle?

Chapter Ten: Take Responsibility

1. Finally, how did Jacob handle conflict with his brother Esau? Read their story in Genesis 32-33? What is your ministry (2 Cor. 5:18-20)?
2. What sin do you justify due to someone's behavior or attitude?
3. What two actions can you take to become healed and righteous to accomplish powerful and effective prayers according to James 5:16?
4. According to 1 Peter 5:5-6, why should you humble yourself?
5. Did you relate to Kirsten and Kylie's story? What is God revealing to you about your part of the conflict in your difficult relationship?

Chapter Eleven: Express Truth in Love

1. Does someone have something against you? If so, what should you do according to Matthew 5:23-24 and James 4:17? How is this affecting your relationship with God and other people?
2. Read Matt. 5:37, what do you say yes to, but really mean no?
3. According to Eph. 4:15, 25 and Matthew 5:13, why speak truth in love?
4. What truth do you need to communicate in love? What are your motives?
5. Using the acrostic ACTS circle the options in the chapter and write down what you will speak in love? Read Gal. 6:1-3, what is God's warning?
6. What lie or false belief is causing dissension in your relationship? Could you relate to Kirsten's struggle with her friend, Pamela, or her husband?

Chapter Twelve: Determine Your Identity

1. What does God say about you? Read Col. 1:27, Psalm 139:8-14; 1 Cor. 2:16; Phil. 4:13; 2 Cor. 5:17.
2. Share how you are healed? Read John 5:1-14. What was your mat? According to Isaiah 53:5 and Psalm 103:1-3 what do you receive?
3. If you struggle with unkind thoughts, judging people, fear, and doubt what is God's promise when you confess it according to 1 John 1:9?
4. How are you involved with your spiritual family? How do you love them?
5. When have you shared your testimony of what God is doing or has done in your life? Have you fallen into the trap of judgment like Jonah did? Jonah saved a city, how can you be obedient to impact generations?

Endnotes

1. Michael R. Pergamit, Ph.D. and Michelle Ernst, Ph.D., "National Runaway Switchboard (NRS) Prevention Curriculum," www.1800runaway.org, April 22, 2010.

2. Dr. Henry Cloud & Dr. John Townsend, *Boundaries,* (Grand Rapids, MI: Zondervan, 1992), 209.

3. Ibid., 140.

4. Mother Teresa, *The Blessings of Love,* (Cincinnati, OH: Servant Publications, 1996), 127.

5. Gavin de Becker, *The Gift of Fear,* (New York, NY.: Dell Publishing, 1997).

6. Gary Chapman, *The Five Love Languages*, (Chicago, IL: Northfield Publishing, 1992).

7. Douglas Stone, Bruce Patton, Sheila Heen, *Difficult Conversations*, (New York, NY: Penguin Books), 37.

8. Robert Bolton and Dorothy G. Bolton, *People Styles at Work and Beyond*, (New York, NY: AMACOM, 2009), 155-218.

9. Dr. Joe S. McIlhaney and Dr. Freda McKissic-Bush, *Hooked,* New science on how casual sex is affecting our children, (Chicago, IL: Northfield Publishing, 2008), 43.

10. Tim LaHaye and Bob Phillips, *Anger Is a Choice*, (Grand Rapids, MI: Zondervan, 1982), 168.

11. Harriet, Lerner, Ph.D., *The Dance of Anger*, A Woman's Guide to Changing the Patterns of Intimate Relationships, (New York, NY: Harper Collins Publishers Inc., 2005), 156.

12. Dr. Neil Anderson, *Victory over the Darkness*, (Ventura, CA, Regal Books, 2000), 208.

13. Dr. James Dobson, *Love Must Be Tough*, (Carol Stream, IL: Tyndale House Publishers, Inc., 1983), 77.

14. Dr. Henry Cloud and Dr. John Townsend, *Safe People*, (Grand Rapids, MI: Zondervan, 1995), 49.

Bibliography

Anderson, Neil T. *Victory over the Darkness,* Ventura, CA: Regal Books, 1990.

Blackaby, Henry T., King, Claude V., *Experiencing God,* Nashville, TN: Broadman & Holman Publishers, 1994.

Bolton, Robert and Dorothy, *Social Style/Management Style,* New York, NY: American Management Association, 1984.

Chambers, Oswald. *My Utmost for His Highest,* Grand Rapids, Michigan: Discovery House Books, 1992.

Chapman, Gary. *The Five Love Languages,* Chicago, IL: Northfield Publishing, 1992.

Cloud, Dr. Henry, Townsend, Dr. John. *Boundaries,* Grand Rapids, MI: Zondervan, 1992.

De Becker, Gavin. *The Gift of Fear,* New York, NY: Dell Publishing, 1997.

Dobson, Dr. James. *Love Must Be Tough,* Carol Stream, IL: Tyndale House Publishers, Inc., 1983.

LaHaye, Tim, Phillips, Bob. *Anger Is a Choice,* Grand Rapids, MI: Zondervan, 1982.

Lerner, Ph. D, Harriet. *The Dance of Anger, A Woman's Guide to Changing the Patterns of Intimate Relationships,* New York, NY: Harper Collins Publishers Inc., 2005.

Mother Teresa, *The Blessings of Love,* Cincinnati, OH: Servant Publications, 1996.

McIlhaney Dr. Joe S., McKissic-Bush, Dr. Freda. *Hooked, New science on how casual sex is affecting our children,* Chicago, IL: Northfield Publishing, 2008.

Morris May, Sharon, PhD. *How to Argue So Your Spouse will Listen,* Nashville, TN: Thomas Nelson, Inc., 2007.

Murray, Andrew. *The Power of the Blood of Jesus,* New Kensington, PA: Whitaker House, 1993.
Humility, Bethany House, Minneapolis, MN: 2001.

Nouwen, Henri. *The Inner Voice of Love,* New York, NY: Image Books Doubleday, 1996.

Packer, J.I. *Knowing God,* Downers Grove, Ill:, Inter Varsity Press, 1973.

Pergamit, Ph.D. Michael R. and Ernst, Ph.D. Michelle, "National Runaway Switchboard (NRS) Prevention Curriculum," www.1800runaway.org, April 22, 2010, 1.

Sande, Ken. *The Peace Maker, A biblical guide to resolving personal conflict.* Grand Rapids, MI: Baker Books, 1991.

Stanley, Charles. *When the Enemy Strikes, The keys to winning your spiritual battles*, Nashville, Tennessee: Thomas Nelson, 2004.

Stone, Patton, and Heen, *Difficult Conversations*, New York, NY: Penguin Books.

Yohannan, Dr. K.P. *Destined to Soar*, Carrollton, TX: gfa books, 2009.

About the Author

Kirsten Strawn, The Faith Coach, Evangelist, and Bible teacher testifies to the resurrection power of Jesus. She ministers God's love and boldly shares His truth to set people free to live the abundant life God has for them. Kirsten and her husband Mark have been miraculously married for over 28 years. They have seen the hand of God heal their marriage, provide during a year without income, heal their five-year-old son from a rare form of leukemia, and guide and direct their path as they raised four determined teenagers. Kirsten and Mark live in beautiful San Diego, California, praising God for His faithfulness.

Thank you for investing your time to read *Loving the Unlovable*. I pray that you have been blessed by the testimonies shared and the transforming truth of God's Word. Please let me know how it impacted your life. Do you have a testimony to share or a prayer request? I would love to hear from you. To grow deeper in your relationship with God, to gain hope in the midst of your struggles, or to contact me visit www.TheFaithCoach.com.

Dear Friend,
My heartfelt prayer is that God fill you and me with the knowledge of His will through all spiritual wisdom and understanding to live a life worthy of the Lord and please Him in every way: bearing fruit in every good work, growing in the knowledge of God, being strengthened with all power according to His glorious might so that we may have great endurance and patience, and joyfully give thanks to the Father, who has qualified us as saints to share in His inheritance. For He has rescued us from the dominion of darkness and brought us into the kingdom of the Son He loves, in whom we have redemption, the forgiveness of sins through the blood of Jesus. That together we can proclaim how wide and long and high and deep the love of Christ by our love for others in Jesus' name. Amen. (Col. 1:9-14, Eph. 3:17-19)

Made in the USA
Middletown, DE
24 October 2016